Pop Quiz

What's *your* country music IQ? Brush up on your TNN trivia and test your knowledge with hundreds of questions about the lives, careers, and music of some of today's hottest country stars. Are you a country music maven? Try these:

- When Kenny Chesney first moved to Nashville, what did he do to earn a living?

- Who was Trisha Yearwood's first musical idol?

- What was the first song Bryan White ever learned?

- What did LeAnn Rimes sing at her first public appearance, when she was only five?

You'll find these answers and hundreds more in the only pop quiz you actually *want* to take! Good luck!

Look for other celebrity biographies from Archway Paperbacks

POP QUIZ
COUNTRY MUSIC

NANCY KRULIK

AN ARCHWAY PAPERBACK
Published by POCKET BOOKS
New York London Toronto Sydney Tokyo Singapore

AN ARCHWAY PAPERBACK *Original*

An Archway Paperback published by
POCKET BOOKS, a division of Simon & Schuster Inc.
1230 Avenue of the Americas, New York, NY 10020

Copyright © 1999 by Nancy Krulik

ISBN: 0-671-03286-0

First Archway Paperback printing August 1999

10 9 8 7 6 5 4 3 2 1

AN ARCHWAY PAPERBACK and colophon are registered trademarks of Simon & Schuster Inc.

Front cover photo credits: Shania Twain © Steve Granitz/Retna; LeAnn Rimes © Ross Pelton/Retna; Dixie Chicks © Steve Granitz/Retna; Bryan White © Brian Smith/Outline Press Syndicate

Printed in the U.S.A.

IL 4+

For Sarah and Emily

Contents

CONTENTS

CONTENTS

What Is Country Music?

Most people say that country music officially became a genre of music in the 1920s. But that's really just when record companies started making what they called "country records," in the hopes of selling music to more rural areas. In reality, people had been fiddling, guitar picking, and singing songs about their day-to-day tears and triumphs for years before the record companies latched on to the sound.

It's hard to define country music. After all, there are a lot of sounds that fit under that heading. Think about it. There's old-time country, honky-tonk, western swing, Cajun country, folk country, country rock, country pop, and much more. But the legendary Hank Williams may have put his finger on the real meaning of country when he declared, "There ain't nothing phony about it. When a folk singer sings a sad song, he's sad. He means it. The tunes are simple and easy to remember, and they're sincere. . . . A [country] song ain't nothin' in the world but a story wrote with music to it."

That just about says it all.

Country music may have started in rural areas as "hillbilly" music, but today its popularity spans the globe. The Grand Ole Opry now attracts an international crowd. And while the older stars still pack the house, the newer stars are bringing a younger audience with them. A whole new generation is being introduced to "America's Music"! The new fans are *buying* country, too. Country music accounts for more than 2 billion dollars in record sales every year!

Country fans are some of the most loyal in the world, and it's easy to understand why. Country songs are so personal. With each lyric, a country singer lets you into a little secret about his or her life. The stars start to feel like family.

So just how much do you know about country music? You're about to find out. The pages of this book are filled with questions about the lives, careers, and music of some of today's hottest country stars. It's up to you to come up with the answers. But just in case a few of the tough ones stump you, we've given you all the answers—just check at the end of each section.

Okay, here goes. Turn the page and let the country fun begin!

Alabama

No act in country music today has a résumé quite like Alabama's. Just look at their stats: 42 number-one hits, 58 million albums sold worldwide, and more than 200 major industry awards!

But the greatest thing about Alabama doesn't show up on their résumé. What is really terrific about this band is that lead singer Randy Owen, bass player Teddy Gentry, multi-instrumentalist Jeff Cook, and drummer Mark Herndon haven't changed despite their popularity. They are still great guys who feel loyal to the fans.

"I think people look for authenticity," Randy says. "You have got to be what you appear to be."

What the members of Alabama appear to be are four buddies who love country music, and who want to make every live performance a party and every song a classic. Maybe that's why no matter

3

where their fans may live, they say, "My home's in Alabama!"

1. Alabama is second to only one legendary country star in having the most number-one records of all music. Name the star who remains at the top of the list.
2. How are Randy and Teddy related?
3. What was Alabama's first number-one hit?
4. *For the Record* is a collection of what?
5. Which Alabama song appears on the sound track of the Patrick Swayze movie *Roadhouse?*
6. The Academy of Country Music named Alabama the artist of what decade?
7. Where did Randy and Teddy grow up?
8. Who are the Singing Owens?
9. What is June Jam?
10. True or false: When the guys were just starting out, they played mostly rock and pop music.
11. Where is the Alabama Theater located?
12. Name Jeff's brand of handmade amplifiers.
13. Finish this lyric from "Mountain Music":
    Drift away like Tom Sawyer,
    ride a raft like Ol' Huck Finn.
    Take a _____.
14. Name the three instruments Jeff plays.

15. Who was Alabama's first drummer?

16. Jeff graduated from Gadsen State Technical College with a degree in what?

17. Finish the name of this Alabama album: *Dancin' on the* _____.

18. Who was Wild Country?

19. True or false: Alabama was once known as the Alabama Band.

20. Which member of Alabama is an only child?

21. What is the name of Alabama's first album?

22. Which two members of Alabama raise cattle?

23. On which holiday in 1979 did Mark join the band?

24. True or false: Alabama has a star on the Hollywood Walk of Fame.

25. Are there any two members of Alabama who are brothers?

26. Which member of Alabama once painted houses and installed carpet for a living?

27. Alabama once played at what amusement park near Fort Payne, AL?

28. When Alabama was just starting out, they played for seven summers at what South Carolina bar?

29. What was the first award ever won by Alabama?

30. True or false: Jeff is afraid to fly, so the band always travels by bus.

Answers to the Alabama Quiz

1. Conway Twitty
2. They are fourth cousins.
3. "Tennessee River"
4. A collection of Alabama's number-one singles
5. "(There's a) Fire in the Night"
6. The 1980s
7. Lookout Mountain, outside of Fort Payne, AL
8. Randy's family—they sang as a gospel group when Randy was just a kid.
9. The annual Alabama charity concert
10. True—and they sang some country, too.
11. Myrtle Beach, SC
12. Stinger Guitar Amps
13. Nap like Rip van Winkle, doze dreaming again
14. Guitar, fiddle, and vocals
15. Teddy Gentry
16. Electronics
17. *Boulevard*
18. Alabama—Wild Country was one of their early names.
19. True

20. Mark
21. *My Home's in Alabama*
22. Teddy and Randy
23. April Fool's Day
24. True
25. No
26. Teddy
27. Canyonland
28. The Bowery
29. *Cashbox* New Vocal Single of the Year in 1980
30. False

Gary Allan

When Gary Allan was just thirteen, he was busy spending his nights playing guitar in honky-tonk clubs. He wasn't necessarily earning any cash, but he *was* getting paid. The knowledge and training he received playing in those clubs were priceless.

These days, Gary is playing for huge, sold-out arenas. But his music still has that old honky-tonk flavor. In fact, his band is called the Honky Tonk Wranglers.

Reviewers say if you listen closely, you'll hear strands of George Strait and Merle Haggard coming through in Gary's music. That's some compliment! But Gary humbly describes his music as "country music, plain and simple. No gimmicks."

Works for us!

1. What did *People* magazine call Gary in 1998?
2. What color are Gary's eyes?
3. How old was Gary when he was offered his first recording deal?
4. Name Gary's first single.
5. True or false: Gary was born in Macon, GA.
6. Gary served in which of the armed forces?
7. Gary formed the Honky Tonk Wranglers with whom?
8. Finish this lyric from "It Would Be You":

   If it was a sad song
   It would be a long one.
   If it was a color
   It would be a deep, deep, blue.
   But if we're talking heartache

   _____

9. Name Gary's first top-five single.
10. What is Gary's hobby?
11. What is Gary's favorite Disney character?
12. Who are Tammy and Greg?
13. True or false: Gary couldn't get a date for his prom.
14. What song did Gary contribute to the sound track of the movie *Black Dog*?
15. Who are Dallas, Tanna, and Maggie?

Answers to the Gary Allan Quiz

1. Sexiest Country Star of the Year
2. Blue
3. Fifteen—he turned down the offer.
4. "Her Man"
5. False—he was born and raised in California.
6. The army
7. Jake Kelly
8. It would be you
9. "It Would Be You"
10. Surfing
11. Tigger
12. Gary's sister and brother
13. False—in fact, many girls asked him.
14. "Highway Junkie"
15. Gary's daughters

Clint Black

Back in 1988, Clint Black was just another young guy looking for country success in Music City. And let's face it, lots of young finger-pickers line the streets of Nashville. But Clint had that something special. In 1989, he got the chance to prove it, releasing his first single, which shot all the way to number one. Before he knew it, Clint was the recipient of the Country Music Association (CMA) Horizon Award. That award was aptly named, because since that first year, Clint has found many huge successes on his horizon, including more than 20 top-ten hits, and more than 50 major music awards.

Clint is also the envy of many men. After all, he's married to the beautiful blond actress Lisa Hartman Black. Lisa was a famous actress before she ever met Clint, and some of Lisa's artistic talents are rubbing off on her husband. Recently Clint and Lisa co-starred in the TV movie *Still Holdin' On: Cadillac Jack's Story*.

Clint and Lisa share homes in Los Angeles and Nashville. But don't let that LA zip code fool you; Clint promises he hasn't gone Hollywood!

"Country is a state of mind," he assures his fans. "Not a state in the union."

Are you in a Clint Black state of mind? Who isn't?! So why not try your hand at some of these Clint questions?

1. Name Clint's first single.
2. Who did Clint steal his first harmonica from?
3. In what year did Clint drop out of high school to join his brother Kevin's band?
4. How many singles from Clint's first album reached number one?
5. In 1993, which tour did *Playboy* magazine name Concert of the Year?
6. In 1993, Clint and Lisa were among the first performers to entertain troops in what country?
7. What song did Clint contribute to *Common Threads,* the Eagles tribute album?
8. On what TV show did Clint make his acting debut?

9. What was the first video Clint ever directed?

10. At which Super Bowl did Clint perform for a billion people?

11. Finish this album title: *Put Yourself*____

12. Complete this lyric from "A Good Run of Bad Luck":

> I've been to the table and
> > I've lost it all before.
>
> I'm willin' _____.

13. Where was Clint raised?

14. How old was Clint when he was inducted into the Grand Ole Opry?

15. Where was Clint born?

16. Name Clint's duet with Wynonna.

17. How did "Cadillac Jack Favor" earn a living?

18. Clint's big-screen debut was in what film?

19. Which of his songs is Clint most proud of composing?

20. How long did it take *Clint Black: The Greatest Hits* to reach platinum status?

21. Name Clint's duet with Martina McBride.

22. With what famous cowboy did Clint perform his first duet?

23. What is located at 7080 Hollywood Boulevard?

24. When was Clint Black Day proclaimed in Houston, TX?
25. Clint played his first guitar solo on what song?

Answers to the Clint Black Quiz

1. "Better Man"
2. His brother Brian
3. 1978
4. 5
5. Clint and Wynonna's Black and Wy tour
6. Somalia
7. "Desperado"
8. *Wings*
9. "A Good Run of Bad Luck"
10. XXVIII
11. *In My Shoes*
12. And able, always comin' back for more
13. Houston, TX
14. Twenty-nine
15. Long Branch, NJ
16. "A Bad Goodbye"
17. He was a rodeo champ.
18. *Maverick*
19. "A Bad Goodbye"
20. Six weeks
21. "Still Holding On"

22. Roy Rogers
23. Clint's star on the Hollywood Walk of Fame
24. December 12, 1996
25. "Nothin' But the Taillights"

BR5-49

B̲R5-49's "Smilin'" Jay McDowell has a question. He wants to know what mystical powers could arrange for "five guys from all over the country, who all love all-time country music [to] all meet in Nashville at the same time?"

Be it luck or divine intervention, the fact that Chuck Mead, Gary Bennett, Jay McDowell, Shaw Wilson, and Don Herron got together is good news for country music. Critics everywhere say that BR5-49 are on a major mission. "The critics say our mission is to save country music," Jay says. And that seems peculiar to him, because he's not exactly sure what the critics think is wrong with Nashville. All the guys in BR5-49 want to do is make good music.

"Everybody knows real music wins out in the

long run, no matter if it's a year or a decade," Jay says.

So far BR5-49's combination of hardcore honky-tonk, western swing, and hillbilly music is winning where it counts: The fans are packing BR5-49's concerts, their music is causing an uproar in country circles, and the end is nowhere in sight.

How much do you know about these twangcore heroes? Pick up your pencil and find out!

1. Where did BR5-49 get their unusual name?
2. Who plays stand-up bass for BR5-49?
3. Where did Chuck and Gary first meet?
4. What group did Jay play with before joining BR5-49?
5. BR5-49 recently opened for what folk-rock legend?
6. BR5-49 were nominated for a 1998 Grammy in what category?
7. True or false: Don plays the dobro.
8. Which two Nashville Music Awards have BR5-49 won?
9. Shaw describes his hometown of Topeka, KS, as a good place to grow what?
10. True or false: BR5-49 once were known for playing eight-hour sets at Robert's

Western World, a bar and clothing store in Nashville.

Answers to the BR5-49 Quiz

1. The name comes from the punch line of a joke from the TV show *Hee Haw* about a really dumb used-car salesman who forgets to put his entire phone number on a billboard.
2. "Smilin'" Jay McDowell
3. The famous Bluebird Cafe in Nashville
4. Hellbilly
5. Bob Dylan
6. Best Country Pop Performance
7. True
8. 1996 Best Country Group/Duo; 1997 Best Country Album *BR5-49*
9. Potatoes
10. False—but the group's energy-packed sets at Robert's did last as long as five hours.

Brooks & Dunn

Both Leon Eric "Kix" Brooks and Ronnie Gene Dunn had successful songwriting careers long before they ever met. But the guys' true success has come as performers. As the singer-songwriter duo Brooks & Dunn they've created a musical sensation, selling more than 14 million albums and winning a truckload of awards—including becoming the only duo in history to be named Entertainer of the Year by the Academy of Country Music and the Country Music Association!

How much do you know about this dynamic duo? Here's your chance to find out.

1. Kix grew up down the street from what famous performer?
2. Why was Ronnie thrown out of his religious college?

3. Who introduced Ronnie and Kix?
4. Name Brooks & Dunn's first album.
5. Which member of Brooks & Dunn likes tennis and art?
6. Brooks & Dunn are the third most successful duo of all time. Who beat them out for the title?
7. Who is Janine?
8. Name Kix's wife.
9. What was Kix's solo single called?
10. For five years in a row Brooks & Dunn won the same Country Music Association award. Name it.

Answers to the Brooks & Dunn Quiz

1. Johnny Horton
2. He wouldn't stop playing in honky-tonks.
3. Arista Records president Tim DuBois
4. *Brand New Man*
5. Ronnie
6. Simon and Garfunkel (first place), Hall and Oates (second place)
7. Ronnie's wife
8. Barbara
9. "When Your Heart Breaks Down" (The single made it to number 73.)
10. Vocal Duo of the Year

Garth Brooks

If country music made its way back to the forefront of the American music scene in the 1990s (which is, of course, where it has always belonged!), the man responsible for the renaissance was none other than Garth Brooks.

Garth Brooks is Oklahoma—born and bred. He's true country, and that's what his fans love about him. Garth's really just one of the people: He's happily married to his college sweetheart, he's the proud papa of three little girls, and he's remarkably humble about his success.

Rather than asking what honors Garth has won, it would be more fitting to try to find some that he hasn't. The truth is, Garth is a music industry unto himself. Not only has he won every major music award, his sales are overwhelming. Consider this: He's the only solo artist to have three albums sell more than 10 million units *(No Fences, Ropin' the Wind,* and *The Hits)*. He's also sold more albums in America than any individual artist in any genre! His elaborate guitar-smashing concerts are standing-room-only parties, and not just in traditional country territory—he's sold out stadiums faster than U2 in their native Ireland, and he attracted the largest crowd ever assembled in Central Park for his 1997 concert.

Garth's broken a lot more records, too, but if we name them we'll be giving away the answers to some of the following questions. And answering questions is your job!

1. Garth's first album sold only 500,000 in its first year. Name it.
2. True or false: Garth is the eldest of the six Brooks children.
3. True or false: Garth did not play guitar until he entered high school.
4. Who is Garth's musical idol?
5. In 1998 Garth made a million-dollar donation to what Nashville tourist attraction?
6. Garth was only the third person in history to serve as host and musical guest on an episode of what TV show?
7. What award did Blockbuster Entertainment bestow upon Garth in March 1998?

8. What Garth song is on the *Hope Floats* sound track?

9. *Garth Brooks Double Live* broke what record its first week of sales?

10. For whom did Garth fill in at the 1998 *Billboard* awards?

11. Where did Garth go to college?

12. What is Garth's full name?

13. Finish this lyric from "That Summer":
    She had the need to feel the thunder
    To clasp the lightning from the sky.
    To watch a storm with all its wonder
    _____.

14. With whom did Garth light the 1998 Christmas tree in Rockefeller Center?

15. In what year did Garth sing the national anthem at the Super Bowl?

16. On what day did Garth sign his contract with Capitol Records?

17. Name Garth's first top-ten hit.

18. Where did Garth grow up?

19. Garth holds a college degree in what?

20. Where did Garth play his first professional gig?

21. Name Garth's three daughters.

22. Garth recorded "Hard Luck Woman" with what rock group?

23. Which of Garth's songs is about domestic violence?

24. Who is Sandy Mahl?

25. True or false: Garth's mom was a country singer.

26. What singing piano man performed with Garth at his concert in Central Park?

27. Which of Garth's songs supports gay rights?

28. What were the names of Garth's first two highly rated NBC specials?

29. How many brothers does Garth have?

30. Name Garth's seventh album (not counting his Christmas album and his advertising promos)

31. What four sports did Garth play in high school?

32. Garth's sister Betsy plays acoustic guitar and sings back up for what group?

33. *The Hits* was originally sold in what food chain?

34. Name Garth's first Christmas album.

35. What is Garth's zodiac sign?

36. Garth earned a partial college scholarship for which sport?

37. What Garth tune did Barry Manilow record?

38. What did Garth's dad do for a living?

39. In what year did Garth break the record for the biggest, fastest-selling concert tour ever fronted by a country act?

40. What is Garth's favorite book?

Answers to the Garth Brooks Quiz

1. *Garth Brooks*
2. False—he's the youngest.
3. True
4. George Strait
5. The Nashville Children's Zoo, which will be named for Mae Axton
6. *Saturday Night Live*
7. Artist of the 1990s
8. "To Make You Feel Love"
9. Most units sold in a week—more than one million
10. Madonna
11. Oklahoma State University
12. Troyal Garth Brooks
13. In her lover's eyes
14. First Lady Hillary Clinton
15. 1993
16. June 17, 1998
17. "Much Too Young (To Feel This Damn Old)"
18. Yukon, OK
19. Advertising
20. Shotgun's Pizza Parlor in Norman, OK
21. Taylor Mayne Pearl, August Anna, Allie Colleen
22. Kiss
23. "The Thunder Rolls"

24. Garth's wife
25. True—she appeared on the *Ozark Jubilee* show in the 1950s.
26. Billy Joel
27. "We Shall Be Free"
28. *This Is Garth Brooks* (1992), *This Is Garth Brooks, Too!* (1994)
29. Four
30. *Sevens*
31. Football, basketball, baseball, and track
32. Stillwater (Garth's band)
33. McDonald's
34. *Beyond the Season*
35. Aquarius
36. Javelin
37. "If Tomorrow Never Comes"
38. He was a draughtsman for an oil company.
39. 1993
40. The Bible

Tracy Byrd

Texas, they say, does everything in a really big way. And that includes creating some of the biggest stars in country music: Tracy Byrd's Texas birthplace can boast of being not only Tracy's hometown, but that of George Jones and Mark Chestnutt, as well! (We're not telling you the name of this music town, you'll have to answer that one yourself in question number four.) You can definitely hear George's and Mark's honky-tonk influences in Tracy's music, as well as some styling borrowed from Lyle Lovett and Gene Watson.

How much do you know about the man who has become one of the great balladeers in country music? Take a Byrd's eye view of this quiz, and find out!

1. Who was the only person Tracy would sing for when he was a child?
2. What Academy of Country Music award did Tracy win for "The Keeper of the Stars"?
3. What is the Tracy Byrd Homecoming Weekend?
4. Where was Tracy born?
5. What was the very first song Tracy recorded in a studio?
6. True or false: As an infant, Tracy was onstage at the Grand Ole Opry.
7. Why did Tracy say he became a George Strait fan?
8. How many weeks did "No Ordinary Man" spend on the charts?
9. What are Tracy's three favorite hobbies?
10. Name Tracy's children.
11. For what paralyzed bull riding champion did Tracy host a benefit concert?
12. Which of Tracy's tunes is one of the most often used wedding songs ever?
13. How high did "Holdin' Heaven" go on the charts?
14. What color are Tracy's eyes?
15. Who is Tracy's favorite singer?

Answers to the Tracy Byrd Quiz

1. Himself
2. Song of the Year
3. A golf and fishing tournament that benefits charities in the Beaumont, TX, area
4. Beaumont, TX
5. "Your Cheatin' Heart"
6. False—but he was in the audience when he was just six months old.
7. Because he brought back the traditional country sound
8. 134 weeks
9. Hunting, fishing, and golfing
10. Eve Elisabeth (Evee) and Logan Lynn
11. Jerome Davis
12. "The Keeper of the Stars"
13. All the way to number one
14. Brown
15. Tag Lambert of Bob Wills and His Texas Playboys

Deana Carter

Deana Carter may seem like an overnight success, but the Music City native assures her fans that's just not true. The fact is, it took Deana ten years to find herself a record deal—which she almost lost when her label, Liberty Records, became Capitol Nashville. Luckily Deana made the final cut on Capitol's artist roster.

Capitol made a wise choice. Deana's voice is golden, or should we say platinum, which both of her CD releases have gone. She's been nominated for top awards, including the Golden Globe and Grammy.

Deana says that she wouldn't trade the years when she was struggling as a waitress for anything—not even real overnight success.

"The crap you go through clears your head instead of clouding it," she insists.

Now it's time for you to pull your head out of the clouds and answer some Deana Carter questions.

1. Who is Deana named for?
2. What did Deana's dad, Fred, do for a living when Deana was growing up?
3. Willie Nelson asked Deana to play at what huge concert, despite the fact that she had no recording contract?
4. At the University of Tennessee, Deana earned a degree in what?
5. According to Deana, the song "Strawberry Wine" reminded her of time spent where?
6. Finish the title of Deana's debut CD: *Did I* _____.
7. How many *Billboard* Hot Country number-one singles were launched from Deana's debut CD?
8. What song did Deana perform on the *Anastasia* sound track?
9. Complete this lyric from "Strawberry Wine":
   We drifted away like the leaves in fall
   But year after year I come back to this place
   Just _____.
10. Name Deana's two dogs.

11. How old was Deana when she first took up guitar?

12. According to Deana, "Music should be like a _____."

13. Who is Deana's husband?

14. How tall is Deana?

15. How does Deana decide which songs to record?

Answers to the Deana Carter Quiz

1. Dean Martin
2. He was a session guitar player.
3. Farm Aid IV—she was the only female to perform in the concert.
4. Rehabilitation therapy
5. Her grandparents' farm
6. *Shave My Legs for This*
7. Three
8. "Once Upon a December"
9. To remember the taste of strawberry wine and being seventeen
10. Gibson and Bet
11. Twenty-three
12. Roller-coaster ride (Deana explains that music "should take you somewhere, be

exciting from start to finish, and then make you want to ride again.")

13. Chris DiCroce

14. 5'6"

15. She chooses songs by what she calls the "goose bump principle": "If I get goose bumps, it's gonna be a hit!" Deana says.

Kenny Chesney

These days, when Kenny Chesney looks up on his shelf, he can see a big shiny Top New Male Vocalist award from the Academy of Country Music. Not bad for a guy who never even thought about being a musician while he was growing up. Kenny was more into sports, especially football—Tennessee football!

Kenny is still a big gridiron fan, but his heart has moved over to music. And boy, are his fans ever grateful!

While no one would call Kenny an overnight success, Kenny says he has built himself a big career "one gold record at a time."

Kenny credits his success to the fact that his music is truth. When it comes to country, Kenny says "the more real, the better. . . . No matter how good a song is, if my heart's not one-hundred percent into it, I just can't make it believable."

Kenny also believes that making music should be fun. Otherwise, what's the point? "I don't know how long the good Lord is gonna let me be in this business, or even be this successful at it," he explains. "So while I'm here, I want to enjoy every minute of it!"

We hope *you* enjoy every minute of this Kenny Chesney quiz!

1. Where did Kenny grow up?
2. True or false: Kenny received his first guitar when he was only five.
3. True or false: Kenny has a college degree in advertising.
4. "Touchdown Tennessee" is Kenny's tribute to what veteran broadcaster?
5. What football player teamed up with Kenny to rerecord "Whatever It Takes" for an NFL country album that benefited the United Way?
6. What was Kenny's first single?
7. True or false: Kenny's dad is a bluegrass singer.
8. When Kenny first moved to Nashville, what did he do to earn a living?
9. Who sings with Kenny on "From Hillbilly Heaven to Honky Tonk Hell"?
10. Name Kenny's first number-one hit.

11. What is Chuckie's Trading Post?
12. What was Kenny's first record label called?
13. Name Kenny's first album.
14. What kind of music did Kenny's mother sing professionally?
15. What is Kenny's favorite song?

Answers to the Kenny Chesney Quiz

1. Luttrell, TN
2. False—he got it in college.
3. True
4. John Ward
5. Peyton Manning
6. "Whatever It Takes"
7. False—he's an elementary school teacher.
8. He parked cars.
9. Tracy Lawrence and George Jones
10. "When I Close My Eyes"
11. A Mexican restaurant Kenny played in while he was in college. He earned twenty dollars a night and dinner.
12. Capricorn Records
13. *In My Wildest Dreams*
14. Gospel music
15. "That's the Way Love Goes" by Merle Haggard

Terri Clark

Who would have thought that a girl from Medicine Hat, Alberta, Canada, would some day travel south of the border down to Music City and take over country music? Terri Clark thought so, that's who! Terri's love of country music has always been a part of her life. She wore Wrangler jeans and cowboy boots all through high school. And although the kids thought that was kind of weird, "They thought it was kind of interesting, too," Terri says.

Those same high school kids voted her most likely to succeed, and they were right! Her first year out, Terri scored three top-five singles, was voted *Billboard*'s top country artist, and saw her first album go gold. (It's since gone platinum, as have her other two albums.)

These days, folks call Terri Clark the singer with

the cowboy hat. But she says that although the hat "is my trademark, I would like to be known for my music rather than what I wear on my head."

Don't worry, Terri. With songs like "If I Were You," "Just the Same," and "Now That I Found You," your music is your legacy!

1. How tall is Terri?
   a. 5'11" b. 6'0" c. 6'1"
2. What did Terri's maternal grandparents—Ray and Betty Gauthier—do for a living?
3. How old was Terri when she picked up her mother's guitar and taught herself to play?
4. What was the first club in Nashville to hire Terri to sing?
5. What did Mercury Records give Terri to celebrate her first gold record?
6. Name Terri's debut album.
7. What instruments does Terri play?
8. What was the name of Terri's CBC Canadian TV special?
9. What toys does Terri collect?
10. What is Terri's favorite color?
11. What color are Terri's eyes?
12. Who did Terri open for on her first major tour?
13. How many years did Terri live in Nash-

ville before getting a contract with Mercury records?

14. True or false: Terri owns a horse named Cupid.
15. True or false: Terri has a whole room in her house dedicated to her fans.
16. Terri works out by participating in what sport?
17. What jeans company recently signed a promotional deal with Terri?
18. How did Terri break her left cheekbone in 1997?
19. True or false: Terri is an only child.
20. Finish this lyric from "If I Were You":
    You know this single life I'm livin'
    Ain't all it's cracked up to be.
    So you're coming to the wrong place
    If _____.

Answers to the Terri Clark Quiz

1. A
2. They were country singers on the Canadian circuit.
3. Nine
4. Tootsie's Orchid Lounge
5. The original window from Tootsie's Orchid Lounge
6. *Terri Clark*

7. Guitar, cowbell, bass, drums, and "anything in the key of C on piano"
8. *Terri Clark: Coming Home*
9. Beanie Babies
10. Forest green
11. Hazel
12. George Strait
13. Eight
14. False—she doesn't own a horse.
15. True—she keeps all her gifts and fan letters in that room.
16. Kickboxing
17. Wrangler
18. She got hit with a softball in a City of Hope charity softball tournament.
19. False—she has a brother, Peter, and a sister, Tina.
20. You want sympathy

Diamond Rio

Marty Roe, Jimmy Olander, Dana Williams, Dan Truman, Gene Johnson, and Brian Prout couldn't have grown up more differently. They hail from all over the country, and their musical influences range from Ella Fitzgerald to the Beatles to the Grand Ole Opry. In fact, before they met at the Opryland amusement park, the only things these guys had in common were a desire to play country music and a love of golf.

But these days, the guys have a lot in common—like their five Grammy nominations, not to mention their millions of loyal fans! (And, oh yeah, they still take time off to play a lot of golf.)

Have you been floating down the Diamond Rio? Take the quiz and discover how much you know about these jewels in the country crown!

1. What was Dan's major in college?
2. When Gene was four years old, he played what instrument at a hometown square dance?
3. Dana is the nephew of which two bluegrass legends?
4. What Opryland band did Dan join in 1985?
5. While they were pitching demo tapes to record labels, where did Marty and Jimmy work?
6. How old was Jimmy when he first met Gene?
7. Who plays drums for Diamond Rio?
8. Name Diamond Rio's 1991 debut album.
9. In 1998 Diamond Rio became the first band in fourteen years to join what fabled institution?
10. Who is the lead singer for Diamond Rio?
11. Who wrote Diamond Rio's "I Thought I'd Seen Everything"?
12. Which Diamond Rio video stars Martin Sheen and his son Ramon Estevez?
13. Diamond Rio's annual golf tournament benefits which charity?
14. Diamond Rio serves as celebrity spokesgroup for what charity?

15. Where did the Diamond Rio guys get the name for their group?
16. Brian knew he was meant to be a musician after watching what British pop group on TV?
17. Marty Roe is named for what country legend?
18. What ride did Marty once operate at Opryland?
19. What is Jim's favorite food?
20. Which member of Diamond Rio once had dinner with Indira Ghandi at her home in India?

Answers to the Diamond Rio Quiz

1. Music composition
2. Mandolin
3. The Osborne Brothers (Bobby and Sonny Osborne)
4. The Tennessee River Boys
5. Cutting grass for the Sunshine Lawn Service
6. Twelve
7. Brian Prout
8. *Diamond Rio*
9. The Grand Ole Opry
10. Marty Roe

11. Huey Lewis and Mutt Lange
12. "It's All in Your Head"
13. The American Lung Association
14. Big Brothers/Big Sisters of America
15. From a Harrisburg, PA, trucking company
16. The Beatles
17. Marty Robbins
18. The Skyride
19. Tuna fish quesadillas
20. Dan Truman

The Dixie Chicks

They're young. They're sexy. They're full of girl power. But don't you dare compare the Dixie Chicks to those other spicy girl singers. For one thing, the Dixie Chicks aren't pop stars, they're classically trained musicians. Martie and Emily spent their childhoods at the symphony, and Natalie was once a student at Boston's acclaimed Berklee School of Music.

Still, with all their classical backgrounds, the Dixie Chicks are pure country. Their unique blue-grass sound is bringing country to the teen market. Girls everywhere are sporting "Chicks Rule" T-shirts and carrying signs that say "I Want to Be a Dixie Chick." (Notice they're not saying "Wanna-be." That's a song by that *other* girl group!)

With a hugely successful CD and several hit

singles, the Dixie Chicks are in the middle of what could be called the ultimate hen party!

1. Name the Dixie Chicks. (First and last names, please.)
2. Which member of the Dixie Chicks does not perform on *Thank Heaven for Dale Evans?*
3. Natalie had the idea for each of the Chicks to have something tattooed onto her ankle every time the group scored a number-one hit. What is it?
4. Which two Chicks are sisters?
5. Which Chick plays the mandolin?
6. The Dixie Chicks got their name from a song by what group?
7. From what state do the Dixie Chicks hail?
8. What was the Dixie Chicks' first number-one hit?
9. Name the two Country Music Association awards won by the Dixie Chicks in 1998.
10. Finish this line from "I Can Love You Better":
    I'm gonna break _____.
11. How old was Emily when she began taking violin lessons?
12. Who is the lead singer of the Dixie Chicks?
13. What place did Martie take at the 1987 Old Time Fiddler Convention?

14. What Tammy Wynette tune did the Dixie Chicks sing at the 1998 Academy of Country Music awards?
15. True or false: Natalie once dyed her hair green.

Answers to the Dixie Chicks Quiz

1. Natalie Maines, Martie Seidel, and Emily Erwin
2. Natalie—the album was recorded before she joined the group.
3. A chicken foot
4. Martie and Emily
5. Martie
6. "Little Feat"
7. Texas
8. "I Can Love You Better"
9. The Horizon Award (for best newcomer) and Vocal Group of the Year
10. This spell she's got on you
11. Seven
12. Natalie
13. Second place
14. "Stand By Your Man"
15. False—but she did once dye it blue.

Vince Gill

Even if you've never bought a Vince Gill CD, or heard a Vince Gill song (we know, that's pretty much impossible to imagine, but bear with us, okay?), you have probably heard Vince Gill perform many, many times. That's because before Vince became one of country's most honored superstars, he was a highly sought-after studio musician, playing guitar and singing backup on albums by artists as diverse as Reba McIntire, Emmylou Harris, and Dire Straits.

Vince was so successful as a studio artist that he wasn't sure he'd ever be a hit on his own. He didn't need to worry. Today, this son of a banjo-playing judge has 10 Grammy awards and 17 CMA awards on his mantel. He's recorded close to 30 top-ten hits and filmed nearly 20 videos!

How much do you know about "the man with

the golden voice"? Take the quiz, and you'll find out!

1. Which song on *The Prince of Egypt* country sound track did Vince write?
2. For whom is "Pretty Little Adriana" written?
3. "When I Call Your Name" reached what spot on the charts?
4. Name Vince's first TV special for CMT.
5. During which war is the "Blue Christmas" video set?
6. With whom did Vince sing "High Lonesome Sound"?
7. What was the name of Vince's high school bluegrass band?
8. Which of Vince's top-ten hits has the same title as a fairy tale?
9. What song won Vince his first Grammy?
10. Name Vince's 1995 hits collection.
11. What career was Vince considering before he decided to become a professional musician?
12. What is Vince's middle name?
13. At what spot on the *Billboard* top country albums chart did *The Key* debut?
14. Where was Vince born?
15. What song did Vince write for his late father?
16. Who is Jenny Gill?

17. How did Vince celebrate his fortieth birthday?
18. What type of music did Vince's former group, Sundance, play?
19. Name the first record Vince ever purchased.
20. In what band did Vince perform with Ricky Skaggs?

Answers to the Vince Gill Quiz

1. "Once in a While"
2. It was written for Adiane Dickerson, a twelve-year-old Nashville honors student who was gunned down.
3. Number one
4. *Song and Verse*
5. World War II
6. Alison Krauss and her band Union Station
7. Mountain Smoke
8. "Cinderella"
9. "When I Call Your Name"
10. *Souvenirs*
11. He wanted to be a professional golfer.
12. Grant
13. Number one
14. Norman, OK
15. "The Key to Life"

16. Vince's daughter
17. He celebrated by performing at the Grand Ole Opry for TNN's *Grand Ole Opry Live.*
18. Bluegrass
19. "They're Coming to Take Me Away, Ha Ha"
20. Doone Creek

Andy Griggs

Even before his self-named debut album was released, Andy Griggs was getting noticed. The press took one look at his video for "You Won't Ever Be Lonely" and went wild—saying that Andy was so sexy, he was like the male version of Shania Twain!

Once the CD hit the shelves, everyone knew that the hype was deserved. Not only does Andy have a face that the camera loves, he has real talent. His music doesn't sound like any other country music out there. "It's really bold and aggressive," Andy says of his sound. "It's in your face."

Which is, apparently, where people want it.

1. Name Andy's debut single.
2. What magazine called Andy a "country Kurt Cobain"?

3. The press got their first good look at Andy in which famous LA nightclub?
4. Andy records for which record label?
5. Where is Andy from?
6. When Andy's father died, which artist's music helped Andy grieve?
7. Who was Mason?
8. Why did Andy learn to play guitar?
9. Who did Andy marry in February 1998?
10. Where was Andy when he found out he had a record deal?

Answers to the Andy Griggs Quiz

1. "You Won't Ever Be Lonely"
2. *TV Guide*
3. The Whisky-a-Go-Go
4. RCA
5. Monroe, LA
6. Merle Haggard
7. Andy's late brother
8. His brother had played guitar, and when he died Andy took it up so he could remain close to him.
9. Stephanie Sullivan
10. He was working in a greenhouse in Nashville.

Wade Hayes

Wade Hayes is a self-proclaimed "shy guy from Oklahoma." But shy might not be the way most people would describe someone who has performed for thousands of people in huge arenas as the opening act for stars such as Tracy Lawrence and Brooks & Dunn. Wade actually seems pretty comfortable onstage. Maybe that's because he never worries about hitting a clinker or forgetting the words in front of an audience. He's got much simpler concerns. "When I go onstage, I just try not to look like a dork," he explains.

Nobody would accuse him of that! In fact, the fans think he's pretty cool—especially the female fans. Wade has become a poster boy in some teen magazines, and he receives literally hundreds of marriage proposals in the mail!

Although Wade is still waiting to be the main

attraction on the bill, he says that opening for some of the best performers in country has its own advantages.

"Every time we do a tour with someone," he explains, "I learn something from them."

Wade is learning his lessons well. He's rapidly becoming one of the hottest acts in the new generation of country stars.

1. Name Wade's debut single.
2. Where is Wade more comfortable—on-stage or in the studio?
3. What is the name of Wade's band?
4. How old was Wade when he began playing lead guitar in his dad's band?
5. What award did Wade win at the 1997 TNN *Music City News* Country Awards?
6. Name Wade's first two back-to-back number-one singles.
7. What song on the CD *On a Good Night* is a tribute to Wade's parents?
8. True or false: All of his life, Wade dreamed of being the lead singer with a country band.
9. What country star hired Wade as a lead guitarist in 1993?
10. Finish this lyric from "I'm Still Dancin' with You":

    When the song was over, I held on a
        little longer,

Deep inside I knew that it was
    wrong.
I could hold her in my arms for the
    rest of the night,
But _____.

11. What is Wade's full name?
12. What is Wade's favorite color?
13. How old was Wade when he got his first real guitar?
14. What is Wade's favorite movie?
15. What is Wade's favorite country song?
16. True or false: Wade has asthma.
17. What kind of motorcycle does Wade ride?
18. What does Wade say is the best advice he ever received?
19. Wade says he has a secret talent. What is it?
20. What two instruments does Wade play?

Answers to the Wade Hayes Quiz

1. "Old Enough to Know Better"
2. Onstage
3. Wheel Hoss
4. Fourteen
5. Male Star of Tomorrow
6. "Old Enough to Know Better" and "I'm Still Dancin' with You"

7. "Our Time Is Coming"
8. False—he wanted to be the lead guitarist for a famous singer.
9. Johnny Lee
10. I'd just be leading her on
11. Tony Wade Hayes
12. Red
13. Eleven
14. *A River Runs Through It*
15. Merle Haggard's "Always on a Mountain When I Fall"
16. True
17. Harley-Davidson
18. Believe in yourself
19. Tiling bathrooms
20. Guitar and mandolin

Faith Hill and
Tim McGraw

According to *Nashville Scene* magazine, you know you're really country if you think of Tim and Faith when you hear the words McGraw Hill. If that's true, then a whole lot of people are country these days.

The Nashville Network's Ralph Emery has dubbed Faith and Tim Mr. and Mrs. Country, and nobody's arguing. Their albums keep selling, the awards keep piling up on the mantel, and Faith and Tim keep going on the road to play directly for the fans.

Touring is truly Faith and Tim's favorite part of the business. This hardworking couple became engaged while on tour, and they've kept their ever-growing family on the move ever since. In 1998, Faith kept performing up until she was eight months pregnant with the couple's second daughter.

But don't think the success has gone to their heads. According to Faith, she and Tim are just everyday folks who are doing what they love. In fact, when she and Tim get a break in touring, all she wants to do is play with the girls and do her laundry!

How much do you know about country's reigning king and queen? Take a leap of faith, and try these questions.

1. What was Faith's job at her very first Country Music Fan Fair?
2. Faith used to sing harmony with Gary Burr at what Nashville Cafe?
3. What is Faith's full name?
4. What color are Faith's eyes?
5. True or false: Faith is afraid of the water.
6. Which two instruments does Faith play?
7. How old was Faith at her first public performance?
8. Name Faith's debut album.
9. Who originally recorded "Piece of My Heart," a song Faith later turned into a huge hit?
10. Where did Tim first propose to Faith?
11. Who is Tim's father?
12. True or false: Tim didn't learn to play guitar until college.
13. Who are Gracie and Maggie?
14. What did Tim sing at his first public appearance?

15. Name Tim's backup group.
16. Name Tim's first top-ten hit.
17. What song does Tim sing on *Faith?*
18. True or false: Faith's *Take Me As I Am* and *It Matters to Me* both went double platinum.
19. Tim's album *Not a Moment Too Soon* went
    a. triple platinum b. quadruple platinum c. quintuple platinum
20. Name Faith and Tim's dogs.
21. Who are Mr. Jeff, Lacy, Dizzie, and Miss Audrey?
22. What was *Billboard*'s best-selling country album in 1994?
23. What do Tim's fans call themselves?
24. In 1997 and 1998 Tim and Faith won back-to-back awards from the Country Music Association. Name the award they won twice in a row.
25. What 1998 CMA awards did Faith and Tim win for "It's Your Love"?

Answers to the Faith Hill and Tim McGraw Quiz

1. She sold T-shirts.
2. The Bluebird Cafe
3. Audrey Faith Perry Hill McGraw

4. Hazel
5. False—in fact, she's really into water-skiing.
6. Guitar and piano
7. Seven—she sang at her first-grade 4H. Club mother-daughter luncheon.
8. *Take Me As I Am*
9. Janis Joplin
10. They were in a dressing-room trailer before a Montana concert.
11. Tug McGraw, a former baseball player for the Philadelphia Phillies
12. True
13. Faith and Tim's daughters
14. "Jesus Loves Me"
15. Dance Hall Doctors
16. "Indian Outlaw"
17. "Just to Hear You Say You Love Me"
18. True
19. C
20. Whitley, Dakota, and Roaddog
21. Tim's horses
22. Tim's *Not a Moment Too Soon*
23. Fun Addicts
24. Vocal Event of the Year
25. Single Record of the Year, Song of the Year, Video of the Year, and Vocal Event of the Year

Alan Jackson

When Alan Jackson signed his first recording contract in 1989, he hoped his career would be huge. Alan definitely got his wish. Just look at the stats: He's sold more than 24 million albums, had 20 number-one hits in six years, and won dozens of awards. Not bad for a southern boy who wasn't sure he could make a living playing music.

But you have to be careful what you wish for. As Alan has learned the hard way, celebrity isn't all it's cracked up to be. Sure, he has the mansion, the motorcycles, the boats, and the planes. But in early 1998, he almost lost the thing that is most precious to him—his family. Alan and his high-school-sweetheart wife, Denise, separated after the strains of fame got to them. In a private matter that became rather public, Alan reluctantly left Denise and the couple's three girls. But before you think this all sounds like another sad country song, relax. It took a lot of work, but Alan and Denise later reconciled, and even renewed their wedding vows.

"(Who Says) You Can't Have It All?"

1. Name Alan's hometown.
2. What was Alan's first number-one album?
3. Where is Alan more relaxed—onstage or in the studio?
4. What is Alan's favorite hobby?
5. What kind of music did Alan sing as a child?
6. Name the first band Alan formed.
7. What did Alan's wife, Denise, do before marrying Alan?
8. Alan once worked in the mail room of what cable network?
9. In what year did Alan become a member of the Grand Ole Opry?
10. Alan is the only artist to win what honor three times in the 1990s?
11. Why did Alan first start wearing a cowboy hat?
12. What is Alan's favorite movie?
13. Name Alan's twin sisters.
14. What is Alan's favorite TV show?
15. Alan's favorite shoes are a pair of custom-

made red cowboy boots that were seen in what video?

16. True or false: As a child, Alan had a pet spider monkey.
17. What kind of motorcycle does Alan collect?
18. Who are the Strayhorns?
19. In 1998, Arista Records released a Spanish version of which of Alan's songs?
20. What eyewear company ran a promotional campaign with Alan for National Safe Boating Week?
21. What restaurant did Alan open in Pigeon Forge, TN?
22. What is Alan's full name?
23. What color are Alan's eyes?
24. What is the first car Alan ever owned?
25. What kind of cowboy hat does Alan wear?

Answers to the Alan Jackson Quiz

1. Newnan, GA
2. *Here in the Real World*
3. In the studio, because as he says, "There aren't ten thousand people staring at you"
4. Fishing
5. Gospel music

6. Dixie Steel
7. She was a flight attendant
8. The Nashville Network
9. 1991
10. ASCAP Songwriter of the Year
11. He has a scar on his forehead that he wanted to cover up
12. Clint Eastwood's *The Outlaw Josey Wales*
13. Cathy and Carol (he also has sisters Diane and Connie)
14. *The Andy Griffith Show*
15. "Chattahoochee"
16. True—his name was Peanuts
17. Harley-Davidson
18. Alan's band
19. "I'll Go On Loving You"
20. Serengeti Eyewear
21. The Alan Jackson Showcar Cafe
22. Alan Eugene Jackson
23. Blue
24. A 1955 Thunderbird convertible
25. A Stetson Rancher

Wynonna Judd

No doubt about it, as far as country music is concerned, the 1980s belonged to the Judds. Starting in 1984 and continuing through the end of the decade, Naomi Judd and her daughter Wynonna sang their way to the top of the charts and into fans' hearts, earning themselves 10 million records and 23 top-ten hits.

The Judds were huge favorites with the fans. And not just because of their music. People simply liked Naomi and Wynonna. Maybe that's because while it was obvious that Naomi and Wynonna had a special relationship, the Judds were unafraid to show that they also had their differences, just like any other mother and daughter. Naomi and Wynonna were also known to be especially hospitable to their fans. And the fans loved the Judds right back.

It seemed as though the Judds could have gone on recording and touring forever. Unfortunately, Naomi was diagnosed with hepatitis (a disease she believes she contracted while working as a nurse years before). After the diagnosis, Naomi decided to put performing on hiatus—but not before one last blowout nationwide tour.

In 1991, Wynonna went solo. Although she admitted at the time that she was afraid of performing without her mom at her side, Wy has done just fine on her own. Not only is she a professional success with plenty of number-one records and big awards to her name; she's found personal joy as well. These days, Wy's a mom. (Isn't it hard to think of beautiful Naomi as a grandmother?!) But don't expect Wynonna to suddenly pack up the leather and the guitars and become June Cleaver. She's more likely to be found riding on her Harley than baking cookies. (Although Wynonna *does* love to cook.)

The best news is yet to come: Word is that Naomi is now well enough to perform, which she and Wy will do together in a special New Year's Eve concert to ring in the new millennium!

Do you know all the F-*WY*-I on Wynonna? Here's your chance to find out.

1. Name the videocassette that follows the Judds across America on the group's final tour.

2. Carl Perkins appears in which Judds videocassette?

3. Who is older—Wynonna or her sister, Ashley?

4. True or false: While touring with the Judds, Wynonna insisted on her own tour bus.

5. On what TV show did Wynonna make her acting debut?

6. Who is Christina Claire Ciminella?

7. In what town was Wynonna born?

8. Wynonna's solo debut CD, *Wynonna,* went

   a. double platinum b. triple platinum c. quadruple platinum

9. Finish this lyric from "I Saw the Light":
   So take your cheating hands off my
       red dress.
   'Cause I ain't wearing this thing for
       you.
   I see you clear now and your lies, too.
   They _____.

10. What star sign is Wynonna?

11. How old was Wynonna when she moved to California?

12. What type of music does Wynonna list as her first influence?

13. Who did the Judds open for at their first show?

14. On what TV show did Wy make her national solo debut?
15. What song did Wynonna sing on the show mentioned in question 14?
16. What song did Wy contribute to the *Tammy Wynette Tribute Album?*
17. What is Wynonna's nickname?
18. How many children does Wynonna have?
19. Who is Wynonna's favorite actress?
20. Name Wynonna's three favorite books.
21. True or false: Wynonna sometimes calls her fans just to chat.
22. With which Judds home video do you get two pairs of 3-D glasses?
23. What song does Wynonna sing on the *Prince of Egypt* sound track?
24. What song did Wy perform on the hundredth episode of *Touched by an Angel?*
25. Who does Wy call "one of the best songwriters in the universe"?

Answers to the Wynonna Judd Quiz

1. *The Farewell Tour*
2. *Their Final Concert*
3. Wynonna
4. False—in fact, the two slept about six feet apart from each other on their bus.

5. *Touched by an Angel*
6. Wynonna—that's her birth name.
7. Ashland, KY
8. C
9. Say that love is blind. But not this time.
10. Gemini
11. Four—she returned to Kentucky when she was ten.
12. Bluegrass
13. The Statler Brothers
14. *The American Music Awards*
15. "She Is His Only Need"
16. "Woman to Woman"
17. Hurricane Wy
18. Two—son, Elijah, and daughter, Grace
19. Her sister, Ashley Judd
20. The Bible, the dictionary, and the *Betty Crocker Cookbook*
21. True—she says, "I call fans on the phone just to surprise 'em."
22. *Love Can Build a Bridge*
23. "Freedom"
24. "Testify to Love"
25. Her mother, Naomi Judd

The Kinleys

The Kinleys have a motto: Two voices, one dream. These days, Heather and Jennifer's dream of being country superstars is coming true. In 1998, their first single, "Please," debuted at number seven on the country charts. That was the highest debut ever from a country music duo. That meant the Kinleys had actually topped one of their favorite duos of all time—the Judds.

In so many ways 1998 was a banner year for the Kinleys. They received several big award nominations, the first of which was from the Grammy people. The Kinleys didn't grab the Grammy, but they did take home an ACM award. (We're not telling which one—that's one of the questions you'll have to answer!)

How much do you know about these terrific

twins? There's only one way to find out. Answer
the questions . . . "Please."

1. How many songs on the Kinleys' debut
   album, *Between You and Me,* feature
   Heather and Jennifer as co-writers?
2. Finish this lyric from "Dance in the
   Boat":
   I can lead the parade
   Or I can stop it.
   Sometimes I _____.
3. Where did Heather and Jennifer grow up?
4. What was the twins' favorite album
   while they were growing up?
5. How old were Jennifer and Heather
   when they moved to Nashville?
6. How did the girls earn money when they
   first arrived in Nashville?
7. What song did the Kinleys contribute
   to *Touched by an Angel: The Album?*
8. What Academy of Country Music award
   did the Kinleys walk home with in 1998?
9. Which twin plays the piano?
10. What old-time crooner does Heather
    think her dad sings like?
11. Both girls have hazel eyes, but one twin
    has a little more brown in hers. Which
    twin is it?
12. How tall are the girls?

13. Heather says that she decided to pick up the guitar after listening to what singer/guitarist?

14. True or false: Heather and Jennifer once auditioned for a Doublemint gum commercial.

15. According to Heather, which of the Kinleys is the more elegant?

Answers to the Kinleys Quiz

1. Five
2. Dance in the boat just to rock it
3. Philadelphia
4. The *Grease* movie sound track
5. Nineteen
6. They were waitresses.
7. "Somebody's Out There Watching"
8. Best New Artist
9. Jennifer
10. Bing Crosby
11. Jennifer
12. 5'7"
13. Bonnie Raitt
14. True—but they didn't get the gig.
15. Heather says Jennifer is more "New York" elegant, and that she is more country.

Patty Loveless

It may be hard to believe that Patty Loveless has been singing professionally for twenty years, but she has the hit singles, platinum albums, and awards to prove it. These days, the poor little girl who listened to the Grand Ole Opry on a radio in her kitchen window—and was once so shy she had to sing for company from another room—is one of Nashville's biggest success stories.

Patty has a love and respect for country music that is sometimes hard to find, and she has never compromised her traditional country roots to find success. Maybe that's what first caught the attention of her Nashville mentors, Porter Wagoner and Dolly Parton.

Patty has a unique bond with her audiences (she overcame her shyness years ago). She knows the folks are there for the music, so she's not the type to make a lot of fancy costume changes during her sets. She just picks up her guitar and sings the songs the people want to hear.

Patty Loveless writes about that traditional country theme: love—and how it affects everyday life. Listening to Patty's music is like having a good talk with an old friend. Sometimes you laugh, sometimes you cry. But you always feel something.

1. What country legend joined Patty on her number-one single "You Don't Seem to Miss Me"?
2. Who was performing at the very first concert Patty ever attended?
3. What was the Country Music Association's Album of the Year in 1995?
4. Patty is the youngest of how many children?
5. What state was Patty born in?
6. What is Patty's newest hobby?
7. Whcrc was the first place Patty ever sang in front of an audience?
8. Who wrote Patty's breakthrough single "I Did"?
9. Patty once had surgery for what?
10. For what song did Patty win the 1998 CMA Vocal Event of the Year award?
11. Complete this lyric from "How Can I Help You Say Goodbye?":

Mama whispered softly,
"Time will ease your pain.
Life's about _____."

12. What was the first band Patty sang with professionally?
13. Which of Patty's albums did the *Nashville Tennessean* call "an album every Nashville artist ought to study"?
14. What did Patty's father do for a living?
15. In what year was Patty inducted into the Grand Ole Opry?

Answers to the Patty Loveless Quiz

1. George Jones
2. Lester Flatt and Earl Scruggs
3. *When Angels Fly* (It was only the second time a woman received the honor.)
4. Seven
5. Kentucky
6. Surfing the Net
7. The Serviceman's Club at Fort Knox. Patty was visiting her older brother Wayne while he was in the army. Her mother bragged that she had a daughter who could really sing, and persuaded Patty to go onstage.
8. Patty Loveless
9. She had an aneurysm removed from her

vocal cords. It was two long, long months before Patty knew whether she would ever sing again.

10. "You Don't Seem to Miss Me"
11. Changing. Nothing ever stays the same.
12. The Wilburn Brothers
13. *The Trouble with Truth*
14. He was a coal miner.
15. 1988

Lyle Lovett

Lyle Lovett may have come to the attention of the masses when he married the movies' pretty woman, Julia Roberts, in 1993, but the country world has known about this Texas son's special brand of music for a long time now. Lyle is the proud owner of no less than five Grammy awards for his country music work.

As his fans well know, Lyle was no stranger to the movies—even before Julia crossed his path. You can hear Lyle Lovett's signature sound on 15 movie sound tracks! Lately, Lyle's been doing his share of on-camera work as well, and his acting has earned him reviews that are almost as glowing as the ones for his music.

Here comes the Lyle quiz—Lovett or leave it!

Bryan White
(B. Gwinn / Retna)

LeAnn Rimes
(Lawrence Marano /
London Features)

Brooks & Dunn
(Nick Elgar / London Features)

Trisha Yearwood
(Jeffrey Mayer / Star File)

The Moffatts
(Anthony Cutajar /
London Features)

Shania Twain
(Mark Harlan / Star Filo)

Faith Hill and
Tim McGraw
(Bill Davila / Retna)

Travis Tritt
(Todd Kaplan /
Star File)

Wynonna Judd
(Todd Kaplan / Star File)

Garth Brooks
(John Spellman /
Retna)

Deanna Carter
(John Lee / Star File)

Martina McBride
(Jeffrey Mayer / Star File)

The Dixie Chicks
(Steve Granitz / Retna)

Vince Gill
(Beth Gwinn /
Retna)

Lee Ann Womack
(Ron Wolfson / London Features)

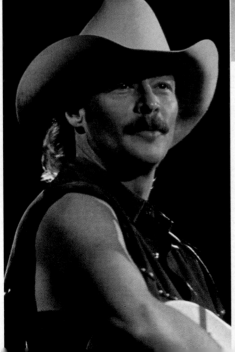

Alan Jackson
(Mitchell Layton / Retna)

1. Who founded Lyle's hometown of Klein, TX?
2. How many years did it take Lyle to graduate from college?
3. Who recorded Lyle's "If I Were the Man You Wanted" on her *Once in a Very Blue Moon* album?
4. In 1989 Lyle won which Grammy award?
5. The songs on *Step Inside This House* are all by whom?
6. How old was Lyle when he began performing?
7. Which two songs from *Lyle Lovett* did Willie Nelson cover?
8. In what Robert Altman film did Lyle make his film debut?
9. Finish this lyric from "She's Leaving Me Because She Really Wants To":
   Say them again
   I need to hear the words once more
   I can't believe how _____.
10. What type of guitar does Lyle play?
11. Finish this song title from a cut from *The Road to Ensenada:* "That's Right ____."
12. How long were Lyle and Julia Roberts married?
13. What profession did Lyle's character have in the film *The Opposite of Sex?*

14. Who sings harmony on "Fiona"?
15. What is the Cycle Shack?
16. What was the name of Lyle's character in *Short Cuts?*
17. What is Lyle's sun sign?
18. What is Lyle's middle name?
19. Which style of cowboy boot does Lyle prefer—pointy-toe or rounded-toe?
20. How long does it take to construct one of Lyle's handmade guitars?

Answers to the Lyle Lovett Quiz

1. Lyle's great-grandfather
2. Six
3. Nanci Griffith
4. Best Male Vocalist
5. Texas songwriters who Lyle says shaped his musical style
6. Eighteen
7. "Farther Down the Line" and "If I Were the Man You Wanted"
8. *The Player*
9. She'll miss me when I'm gone
10. A Collings
11. (You're Not from Texas)
12. Twenty-one months
13. He played a sheriff.
14. Jackson Browne and Shawn Colvin

15. A motorcycle shop where Lyle worked as a teen
16. Andy Bitkower
17. Scorpio
18. Pearce
19. Pointy-toe
20. Thirty-two days

The Lynns

You could call the Lynns the "Coal Miner's Granddaughters." After all, their mom, legend Loretta Lynn, made the song "Coal Miner's Daughter" a country classic. But although Patsy and Peggy Lynn are proud of the legacy their mama has passed down to them, they prefer to be judged on the merits of their own music. In fact, Peggy insists that before being signed to a recording contract, "We didn't tell anyone who our family was. It wasn't an issue. It was all about our music."

And it's their music that has brought them success. According to Patsy and Peggy, the executives at Warner Bros./Reprise Records didn't even know that the twins were Loretta Lynn's daughters until after they'd been signed.

The Lynns have proven that they are true chips off the old Lynn block. Following the release of their hit debut album, *The Lynns,* Patsy and Peggy were nominated for every vocal duo category in country music awards.

The girls think that being twins has contributed to their success. Musically, their voices blend in a way that only family can. But don't kid yourself— while their voices are in perfect harmony, their relationship isn't always.

"We will fight over the time of day," admits Patsy, "but we have never had a cross word with each other musically."

How much do you know about this new generation of Lynn musicians? It's time to find out!

1. How old were the twins when they made their debut at the Grand Ole Opry?
2. Before calling themselves the Lynns, Patsy and Peggy called themselves which of the following:
   a. Loretta's Ladies   b. The Tootsie Twins   c. The Honk-a-Billies
3. "I Won't Leave This World Unloved" is a song based on whose last words?
4. When Patsy and Peggy were three years old, they sang at Tootsie's Orchid Lounge. What did Mrs. Tootsie give them in return?
5. What article of her mother's clothing did Peggy wear onstage in the early years?

6. What was the first song Peggy and Patsy ever sang together?

7. Who came to Nashville first to pursue her musical career—Peggy or Patsy?

8. Who is Patsy named for?

9. Who are Dareen, Megan, and Anthony?

10. Which twin lists sushi as her favorite food?

11. Which twin lists Elvis as her favorite musician?

12. Match the twin to her middle name:
    a. Jean   b. Ilene

13. In 1998, what magazine called the Lynns "the brightest stars to hit country music"?

14. What is the name of the Lynns' fan club newsletter?

15. What is the name of the ranch Peggy and Patsy call home?

16. About which song did Patsy say: "I would love to see the face of that girl when she realizes where she heard those words before"?

17. Which of the songs from the twins' demo tape made it onto *the Lynns?*

18. Who produced *the Lynns?*

19. What is Peggy's favorite song on *the Lynns?*

20. True or false: Loretta Lynn insisted her

twins go to a small boarding school for security's sake.

Answers to the Lynns Quiz

1. Three weeks
2. C
3. The girls' father, Mooney Lynn
4. Coca-Cola and a pack of gum
5. Her boots
6. "All I Have to Do Is Dream" by the Everly Brothers
7. Peggy
8. Patsy Cline
9. Patsy's kids
10. Patsy
11. Peggy
12. Peggy—a; Patsy—b
13. *People*
14. *Honk-a-Billies Quarterly*
15. Hurricane Mills
16. "Woman to Woman"
17. "It Hurts Me"
18. Don Cook
19. "Someday"
20. False—they went to public school like everyone else.

Martina McBride

Looking at petite Martina McBride, you might think you were dealing with a meek little lamb. But you would be fooling yourself. Martina may be tiny, but she's a real tiger.

Martina's voice is strong and powerful, and the things she sings about are powerfully important. Take what might just be her most famous single, "Independence Day." It's about a woman who burns down her house—with her abusive husband inside it. And then there's "Cheap Whiskey," a song about the effects of drunk driving.

Martina says she doesn't necessarily set out to record "issue songs." Instead, she just records the songs that touch her heart. And she refuses to record any song that doesn't reflect her strong moral beliefs. "I've always felt that the people who buy my records are getting a piece of me and something I stand for or believe in," she recently told *Country Song Round Up*. It's a responsibility she doesn't take lightly.

"There have been a lot of times when people have tried to sway me from what I knew I needed to do, but I've learned you have to listen to your instincts," she says. "Only you know what is truly right for you."

1. True or false: Martina was raised in Dallas, TX.
2. Martina once sold T-shirts at a concession stand for a country superstar. She later opened for him on one of his tours. Who is he?
3. What is Martina's favorite season?
4. Who is Delaney?
5. In 1994, Martina won the Country Music Association's Video of the Year award for what song?
6. Who was the major inspiration for *Wild Angels?*
7. Name the first band Martina performed with.
8. True or false: Martina's first hit album was her debut, *The Time Has Come.*
9. What did Martina buy in 1997, to keep it from being torn down?
10. Who are the Penetrators?
11. What is Martina's birth sign?

12. True or false: Martina is a workout fanatic and travels with a personal trainer.
13. What awards show did Martina host with Lorrie Morgan and Mark Miller?
14. Martina's husband John is production manager for what male country artist?
15. Complete this lyric from "Valentine":
    If there were no words
    No way to speak,
    I _____.

Answers to the Martina McBride Quiz

1. False—Martina was born and raised in Sharon, KS (population 200).
2. Garth Brooks
3. Fall
4. Martina's older daughter
5. "Independence Day"
6. Martina's daughter Delaney
7. The Schiffters—her family's band
8. False—her career didn't take off until her second CD, *The Way I Am*.
9. The church she sang in as a child.
10. A cover band Martina sang with in the late 1980s
11. Leo
12. False—she says she doesn't like to work.

out, and really doesn't need to. She's just naturally slim.

13. The TNN *Music City News* Country Awards show
14. Garth Brooks
15. Would still hear you

The Moffatts

They're brothers. They've been singing since they could talk. They have young girls screaming at them wherever they go. Is it any wonder some people call the Moffatts the country Hanson?

The Moffatts differ from Hanson in many ways. For starters, there are four Moffatts, three of which are triplets. (No way are we telling which three—you've got to answer that one yourself!) Second, up until recently the Moffatts were pure country. They moved all the way from Canada to Nashville, just so they could ensure that their sound had just the right twang. These days, the boys have been recording more contemporary pop songs—but their country background comes through in every one.

How much do you know about the amazing Moffatts? It's time to find out!

1. Where in Canada are the Moffatts from?
2. Which three Moffatts are triplets?
3. Which Moffatt is nicknamed Duke?
4. Who is the youngest of the triplets?
5. What is Clint's favorite fast-food place?
6. What is Bob's favorite color?
7. What is Scott's nickname?
8. Finish this lyric to "I'll Be There for You":
   I wanna show you how
      good it will be.
   Never needed anyone
   The way I need _____.
9. Who is the Moffatts' mom?
10. True or false: The Moffatts tour only during school vacations.

Answers to the Moffatts Quiz

1. Vancouver
2. Bob, Clint, and Dave
3. Bob
4. Dave
5. Taco Bell
6. Purple

7. Elvis
8. You right now
9. Country singer Darlana Moffatt
10. False—the boys are home-schooled by their dad, and they can tour whenever they like.

Collin Raye

Collin Raye knows he's lucky. He's living the kind of life others can only fantasize about. Collin also knows that not everyone has the kind of good fortune he has. So Collin spends a great deal of his time alerting his fans to domestic problems, and helping people find ways out of their troubles.

"I've started to look at my job as a ministry," he says. "There's nothing wrong with having a good time, but we always try to make our shows the best of both worlds."

Over the years, Collin has lent his name to countless charity events. He's also alerted his fans to the horrors of spousal and child abuse and alcoholism. He's offered people with problems hope as well, by placing the phone numbers of organizations such as Al-Anon at the end of his videos.

But Collin is fully aware that he is first and

foremost an entertainer. So the songs he sings are thoughtfully chosen, and his live shows are designed to keep his fans satisfied. That formula has paid off—he's won plenty of awards, and his walls are lined with gold and platinum albums.

How much do you know about country's Raye of hope? Check out these questions and you'll find out!

1. How old was Collin when he started performing?
2. What did Collin and his brother, Scott, start after Collin finished high school?
3. Name the group that included Collin, his brother, and his mother.
4. What was Collin's debut album?
5. Collin's "I Think About You" video won the first Music Now award from which Tennessee task force?
6. Which of Collin's albums was one of *USA Today*'s Top 10 Albums of 1991?
7. Which of Collin's songs was written by his ex-girlfriend about their failed love affair?
8. Which of Collin's songs is about alcoholism?
9. How many weeks did "Love, Me" spend at the top of the charts?
10. What 1997 ACM award did Collin win?
11. True or false: Collin is a baritone.
12. What Dallas Cowboys event did Collin co-host?

13. Finish this lyric from "All I Can Be":
    You're young and so beautiful
    And I'm glad I'm here.
    But _____.
14. What is Collin's birth name?
15. Name Collin's kids.

Answers to the Collin Raye Quiz

1. Seven—he sang backup for his mother,
   Lois Wray.
2. A band called the Wray Brothers
3. The Wrays
4. *All I Can Be*
5. The Tennessee Task Force on Domestic
   Abuse gave him the award for raising
   awareness of spousal abuse.
6. *All I Can Be*
7. "I Can Still Feel You"
8. "Little Rock"
9. Three
10. Video of the Year
11. False—he's a tenor.
12. The Dallas Cowboys' Special Teams for
    Special Olympics
13. The ending is painfully clear
14. Floyd Collin Wray, Jr.
15. Britanny and Jacob

LeAnn Rimes

You know you've really made it when everyone knows you by your first name. Say the name LeAnn, and you immediately think of LeAnn Rimes—the seventeen-year-old Texas dynamo who's got platinum albums, awards, hit TV specials, and a best-selling novel to her name.

LeAnn Rimes may not be the first teenager to wow the country world with her amazing voice, but she is definitely today's country "it" girl! She's got what it takes—an amazing voice, songwriting abilities that go far beyond her years, and the uncanny ability to choose songs that people want to hear over and over again.

LeAnn's popularity has not come without a price. She doesn't go to school like other teens, so proms and homecoming dances are pretty much out of the picture. Also, the pressures of constantly being on the road with their daughter added to the strain in LeAnn's parents' marriage, which finally ended in divorce in 1998. (LeAnn says that since the divorce her parents are much happier, and because they're happier, so is she.)

LeAnn has also taken her share of knocks from the Nashville elite. In 1997, she won the Country Music Association's Female Vocalist of the Year and Horizon awards. But by 1998, she'd been shut out of the nominations for the CMA awards. Still, LeAnn took the disappointment in stride.

"I think it's totally political," she told *TV Guide*. "I think my music has nothing to do with me not getting a nomination. I don't record in Nashville. I don't do a lot out there. They expected me to go in [to a Nashville recording studio] and do everything the way everyone else has done it in the past, and I didn't do that."

But don't be totally fooled. LeAnn may be savvy beyond her years, but she's still a teenager who has to be reminded to make her bed on the tour bus, and who has crushes on celebrities like soap opera star Jensen Ackles.

Does LeAnn light up your life? To find out just how much you know about her, start with question number one.

1. What is LeAnn's full name?
2. What are LeAnn's favorite sports?

3. True or false: LeAnn hates math.

4. What did LeAnn sing at her first public appearance, when she was only five?

5. LeAnn says she models her career after that of which country singer?

6. What is LeAnn's favorite soap opera?

7. Which Bryan White song did LeAnn record?

8. Which LeAnn tune can be heard in the animated movie *Quest for Camelot*?

9. Which song by the Artist Formerly Known as Prince appears on LeAnn's album *Sittin' On Top of the World*?

10. True or false: LeAnn won the 1997 Grammy for Best New Artist.

11. LeAnn made her acting debut in which made-for-TV movie?

12. Who co-wrote the novel *Holiday in Your Heart* with LeAnn?

13. True or false: LeAnn was born in Dallas, TX.

14. What does LeAnn's favorite T-shirt say?

15. In what year was LeAnn's first hit, "Blue," released?

16. How old was LeAnn when she signed her first recording contract?

17. True or false: LeAnn likes to stick to the artistic side of her career, leaving the business to her managers.

18. How old was LeAnn when she recorded her first album?

19. Finish this lyric from "How Do I Live":
    Without you there would be no sun
       in my sky
    There would be no love in my life
    There'd be _____.

20. Name LeAnn's contemporary Christian CD.

21. Which of LeAnn's CDs is a compilation of her earlier recordings?

22. LeAnn's CD *You Light Up My Life* reached the top of which three charts simultaneously?

23. LeAnn used to sing the national anthem at sporting events for what team?

24. With what pop music legend did LeAnn record the duet "Written in the Stars"?

25. What is the longest-running *Billboard* Hot 100 single of all time?

26. LeAnn once had two albums in the Country Top 20 at the same time. Name them.

27. How old was LeAnn when she started singing?

28. What car did LeAnn treat herself to for her sixteenth birthday?

29. True or false: LeAnn once dated Bryan White.

30. True or false: In 1997, LeAnn's combined album and ticket sales topped 100 million dollars.

Answers to the LeAnn Rimes Quiz

1. Margaret LeAnn Rimes
2. Softball and baseball
3. False—math is actually her *favorite* subject.
4. "Getting to Know You"
5. Reba McEntire
6. *Days of Our Lives*—LeAnn was lucky enough to appear in a few episodes of the show.
7. "When Am I Gonna Get Over You?"
8. "Looking Through Your Eyes"
9. "Purple Rain"
10. True
11. *Holiday in Your Heart*
12. Tim Carter
13. False—she's originally from Jackson, MS.
14. "I Am Tiger Woods"
15. 1996
16. Thirteen
17. False—in fact, LeAnn says, "I am very involved in the business part of it. I

guess I am making decisions now that are going to affect me for the rest of my life."

18. Eleven—the album *After All* was a small independent release.
19. No world left for me
20. *You Light Up My Life*
21. *Early Years*
22. It topped the country, pop, and contemporary Christian charts, something no other country recording artist has ever accomplished.
23. The Dallas Cowboys
24. Elton John
25. "How Do I Live"
26. *Sittin' On Top of the World* and *You Light Up My Life*
27. Two
28. A Dodge Viper
29. False—they have always been just friends.
30. False—but the sales did reach approximately 96.3 million dollars.

South Sixty-Five

What's that? You say you haven't heard of this country quintet? Well, don't worry, if Brent Parker, Stephen Parker, Doug Urie, Jerimy Koeltzow, and Lance Leslie have anything to say about it, you will! These guys are the newest members of an exclusive club. Call it Country: The Next Generation.

The members of South Sixty-Five were chosen from hundreds of aspiring country artists who answered advertisements for an audition for a new country group. Doug Urie recalls feeling that "getting the callback for my audition has been the most memorable moment in my life, so far."

And although most of the five guys had never met each other—never mind *sung* together—before they met in an Atlantic Records conference room in October 1997, their voices blended almost instantly.

It's been a long time since country music had a band without a lead singer. But these guys believe in equal time. They take turns singing lead on songs like the Oak Ridge Boys–esque "Baby's Got My Number" and the soft ballad "No Easy Goodbye."

South Sixty-Five is hoping that their youth, energy, and talent will introduce a whole new group of young people to country music. So why don't you take a trip down South 65, and answer these questions?

1. South 65 is the name of the interstate highway that runs through which musical city?
2. What member of the pop group All-4-One was instrumental in starting up South Sixty-Five?
3. At which theme park did Lance Leslie work before joining South Sixty-Five?
4. Brent Parker says he hopes he can sell as many albums as what pop group?
5. Who is the youngest member of the group?
6. South Sixty-Five's first single was used as the theme song for what organization?

7. Where was South Sixty-Five's first video, "Random Act of Senseless Kindness," shot?
8. How are Brent and Stephen related?
9. What three instruments does Jerimy play by ear?
10. True or false: All the members of South Sixty-Five play instruments and write songs.

Answers to the South Sixty-Five Quiz

1. Nashville, TN
2. Delious Kennedy
3. Six Flags Fiesta Texas
4. The Backstreet Boys (The South Sixty-Five guys are often compared to this mega-successful pop quintet.)
5. Doug Urie
6. The Random Acts of Senseless Kindness Organization, which has 600,000 members in schools nationwide
7. Montreal
8. They are brothers.
9. Piano, guitar, and drums
10. True

George Strait

Many country crooners have worn cowboy hats, but George Strait has earned his. Not only did he once work for a cattle-pen company, he still ropes cattle.

But ask George if he would give up his singing career for cowboy work, and he'll answer, "That's impossible!"

It's also impossible to imagine the country scene without George Strait. Over the past eighteen years he's released 22 albums—all of which have gone gold, platinum, or multi-platinum. He's also managed to win more than 35 major awards.

How much do you know about the world's most popular singing cowboy?

1. Name George's debut record.
2. What is George's nickname?

3. George starred in which 1992 film?

4. What character did George play in the film named in question number 3?

5. In which state is George's cattle farm?

6. George is really into one cowboy sport. Name it.

7. Which of these stars did not perform at the 1998 George Strait Chevy Truck Country Music Festival: Tim McGraw, Faith Hill, Shania Twain, Lee Ann Womack, or John Michael Montgomery?

8. What is George's wife's name?

9. What is George's son's name?

10. Name George's multi-platinum boxed set.

11. True or false: George would like to record a tribute album to Frank Sinatra.

12. What is the best-selling country boxed set of all time?

13. Which two instruments does George play?

14. Where was George stationed while he was in the army?

15. Which is George's best-selling album to date?

16. What was George's first award for?

17. What color are George's eyes?

18. Name George's college band.

19. George holds a bachelor of science degree in what subject?
20. Name the young boy whose voice you hear on the single "Heartland."
21. The Jennifer Strait Memorial Foundation (named for George's daughter, who died in a car crash at age thirteen) benefits what types of charities?
22. Finish this lyric from "Baby Blue":
    She always held it deep inside
    But somehow I always knew she'd

    _____.

23. Where was George born?
24. True or false: George is a huge fan of rapper Bobby Brown.
25. What year was George voted Best-dressed Man in Country Music by the readers of *Music City News?*
26. What album did the Ace in the Hole band first play on?
27. George was the first person to wear a cowboy hat on what show?
28. Name George's first live video.
29. What is George's middle name?
30. When roping, would George rather be the header or the heeler?

Answers to the George Strait Quiz

1. *Unwound*
2. Gorgeous George
3. *Pure Country*
4. Dusty Chandler
5. Texas
6. Team roping
7. Shania Twain
8. Norma
9. George Jr. (his nickname is Bubba)
10. *Strait Out of the Box*
11. True
12. *Strait Out of the Box*
13. Guitar and piano
14. Hawaii
15. *Pure Country*
16. *Billboard*'s New Male Artist Album of the Year (1981)
17. Green
18. Stoney Ridge
19. Agriculture
20. George's son, Bubba
21. Charities that support children in need
22. Go away when the grass turned green
    And the sky turned baby blue
23. Poteet, TX
24. False—but he *is* a big fan of Bobby's wife, Whitney Houston.

25. 1987
26. *Ocean Front Property*
27. *Hee Haw*
28. *George Strait Live*
29. Harvey
30. He says he'd rather heel.

Thrasher Shiver

It's been said that if the 1980s belonged to the Judds, and the 1990s belonged to Brooks & Dunn, then the millennium is the property of the red-hot duo Thrasher Shiver.

That comes as no surprise to the two men who join their voices to create the award-winning duo.

"Our style is different than that of other duos," Kelly Shiver says.

Neil Thrasher agrees, explaining that rather than having the usual lead singer and harmony man, "We're like one voice."

That different duo sound has paid off big time for Thrasher Shiver. In 1997 they were named the ABC Radio Network's New Act of the Year. They've also been nominated twice for the CMA's Vocal Duo of the Year award.

Can you thrash your way through these Thrasher Shiver questions?

1. Neil's dad was a member of what gospel group?
2. Who was once in a band called County Line—Neil or Kelly?
3. Who sang on Garth Brooks's *No Fences*—Neil or Kelly?
4. How old was Kelly when he began writing songs?
5. True or false: Neil and Kelly wrote songs together before they sang together.
6. Name Neil and Kelly's debut CD.
7. Who introduced Neil and Kelly?
8. What is Kelly's wife's name?
9. What veteran producer did Kelly and Neil hire to help produce their debut album?
10. Thrasher Shiver performed on the sound track for what Bill Paxton film?
11. Who is older, Kelly or Neil?
12. Before joining Thrasher Shiver, Kelly played with a band that performed in what Tennessee town?
13. Neil says he got some of his best stage experience from doing what?
14. Finish this lyric from "All the King's Horses":

And all the king's horses, and all the
king's men,
Could never _____.

15. Which of the following do Kelly and
Neil not list as one of their hobbies?
a. fishing   b. golfing   c. waterskiing

Answers to the Thrasher Shiver Quiz

1. The Thrasher Brothers
2. Kelly
3. Neil
4. Nine
5. True
6. *Thrasher Shiver*
7. Their manager, Bob Doyle
8. Kelly
9. Justin Niebank
10. *Traveler*
11. Kelly, by two years
12. Savannah
13. Performing at age eighteen with his
dad's band
14. Put you and what's left of me back
together again
15. C

Pam Tillis

On first meeting, Pam Tillis may seem a little spacy. But don't fool yourself; Pam's brain is constantly working.

"Artists are so seemingly absentminded," she admits. "When we are not in the studio or on-stage, we're just walking around and in the process of making something."

And what Pam Tillis has been in the process of making is a red-hot country music career that is worthy of some of the old-time country greats—like her dad, Grand Ole Opry legend Mel Tillis. Pam's résumé is filled with honors—gold and platinum albums, 15 top-ten hits, and a CMA Female Vocalist of the Year award. And she's managed to do all that while hosting TV specials on the TNN network. Who says "all the good ones are gone"?

How much can you tell us about Tillis? Take the quiz and find out!

1. What story did Pam narrate for the *Froggy's Country Cassette* series?
2. What do Pam's singles "Don't Tell Me What to Do," "When You Walk in the Room," and "Mi Vida Loca" have in common?
3. True or false: Pam is the youngest of Mel Tillis's five children.
4. True or false: Pam was born and raised in Nashville.
5. Pam's first turn as sole producer came on which album?
6. Who co-wrote "Tequila Mockingbird" with Pam?
7. With which symphony orchestra did Pam perform in 1998?
8. True or false: Pam has never performed with her dad.
9. True or false: Pam won the CMA Horizon Award in 1992.
10. What speech impediment does Pam's dad have?
11. What British 1960s pop group does Pam list among her influences?
12. In what year did Pam first win the CMA's Female Vocalist of the Year award?
13. What type of clothing does Pam collect?

14. Who is Ben DiPiero?
15. Finish this lyric from "Mi Vida Loca":
I go where the wind blows.
You can't _____.

Answers to the Pam Tillis Quiz

1. "Goldilocks and the Three Bears"
2. They all reached number one on the country charts.
3. False—she's Mel's eldest.
4. False—she was born in Plant City, FL, and raised in Nashville.
5. *All of This Love*
6. Her brother, Mel Tillis, Jr.
7. The St. Louis Symphony Orchestra
8. False
9. False—but she was nominated for the award.
10. He stutters.
11. The Beatles—Pam even performed the group's "Got to Get You Into My Life" during her performance with the St. Louis Symphony.
12. 1994
13. Jackets
14. Pam's son
15. Tame a wild rose

Randy Travis

Music saved Randy Travis's soul. It probably saved his hide, too, since his performing ability kept him away from a long jail stretch. As a teenager, Randy was more into drinking and drugging than anything else. He'd been convicted of drug- and alcohol-related crimes when he was discovered by North Carolina club owner Lib Hatcher, who had Randy released into her custody before he was shipped off to prison. Lib made sure Randy cleaned up his act, and then became his manager.

Randy Travis became the ACM's Top New Male Vocalist in 1985, and went on to define the new country sound in the 1980s with songs like "On the Other Hand" and "Forever and Ever, Amen." In his first ten years as a superstar, Randy sold 20 million records and placed 25 singles in the top ten. It's no surprise that folks say he paved the way for artists like Garth Brooks and Alan Jackson.

Randy's also been a huge hit on the big and small screens, starring in films and made-for-TV movies. It seems there's nothing this man can't do!

Are you a Randy expert? Take this Travis test and find out!

1. Randy was the first country artist to sign with which label?
2. What is Randy's real name?
3. In what year did Randy move to Nashville?
4. At what Nashville club did Randy wash dishes?
5. What was the first debut album by a solo male country artist to go platinum in less than a year?
6. True or false: In 1986, Randy became the youngest star ever to be asked to join the Grand Ole Opry.
7. In what Bruce Dern film did Randy appear?
8. How many years does Randy say it took him to make it in music?
   a. 10   b. 7   c. 5
9. What color are Randy's eyes?
10. What is Randy's favorite movie?

11. Randy once performed atop which Disneyland attraction?
12. What is Randy's all-time favorite country song?
13. The video for "Spirit of a Boy, Wisdom of a Man" was shot where?
14. Name Randy's first film.
15. Randy appeared in "The Adventures of Rudy Kazootie," an episode of what TV show?
16. With whom did Randy first perform at age ten in VFW halls?
17. True or false: Randy once appeared on the *Andy Griffith Show*.
18. What is Randy's favorite meal?
19. Finish this lyric from "I Told You So":
    I told you so, but you had to go
    Now I've found somebody new
    And you _____.
20. True or false: There is a whirlpool on Randy's tour bus.

Answers to the Randy Travis Quiz

1. DreamWorks SKG
2. Randy Bruce Traywick
3. 1981
4. The Nashville Palace
5. *Storms of Life*

6. True
7. *Dead Man's Revenge*
8. A
9. Blue
10. *Lonesome Dove*
11. The Matterhorn
12. "He Stopped Loving Her Today"
13. At the offices of the *Herald Examiner* in Los Angeles
14. *Young Guns*
15. *Sabrina the Teenage Witch*
16. His brother Ricky
17. False—but he did appear on Andy's *Matlock* series.
18. Home-cooked vegetables
19. Will never break my heart in two again
20. True

Travis Tritt

Back in the early 1990s, cowboy hats were the signature of the new male country stars. Garth Brooks had one; so did Clint Black and Alan Jackson. But Travis Tritt left his hat at home. And that small act of rebellion was nothing compared to the actions that were to come. Before long, country's new bad boy was riding motorcycles onto the stage and adding raucous rock beats to his country tunes.

These days Travis is a married man and a father. But don't kid yourself—he hasn't suddenly settled into some *Leave It to Beaver* wholesome daddy type. While marriage may have tamed his roving eye for the ladies, it hasn't tamed his music. He says he's still writing "stuff that tends to put some drive in your country."

Drive on, Travis!

1. Finish the title of one of Travis's biggest hits: "Here's a Quarter _____."

2. Which of these movies did Travis not perform in: *The Cowboy Way, Scream,* or *Sgt. Bilko?*

3. Travis performed at the Super Bowl halftime show in what year?
   a. 1993   b. 1994   c. 1995

4. What is Travis's middle name?

5. What kind of motorcycle does Travis ride?

6. What is painted on the side of Travis's tour bus?

7. Name Travis's first single.

8. What kind of cars does Travis race?

9. Name the five songs on the *It's All About to Change* video.

10. For what label does Travis record?

11. Where was Travis born and raised?

12. Where did Travis go to college?

13. What breed of horse does Travis raise?

14. Which of the following does Travis not list as an influence: John Denver, George Jones, Lynyrd Skynyrd, or Johnny Cash?

15. What is the name of Travis's autobiography?

16. What's Travis's daughter's name?

17. True or false: Travis's dad was very

supportive of Travis's professional music dreams.

18. Which two singers appeared in the made-for-TV movie *The Long Kill* with Travis?

19. What was the first album Travis ever produced?

20. Who shared the bill with Travis on the Double Trouble tour?

Answers to the Travis Tritt Quiz

1. (Call Someone Who Cares)
2. *Scream*
3. A
4. Travis (His real name is James Travis Tritt)
5. Harley-Davidson
6. Les Paul Standard Guitars
7. "Country Club"
8. Super Comp hot rods
9. "Country Club," "Help Me Hold On," "Drive in Your Country," "Drift Off to Dream," "Here's a Quarter (Call Someone Who Cares)"
10. Warner Bros.
11. Marietta, GA
12. Travis didn't go to college.
13. Appaloosa

14. Johnny Cash
15. *Ten Feet Tall and Bulletproof*
16. Tyler Reese Tritt
17. False—as Travis says, "My dad thought music was something you sang around the house. It definitely wasn't something you pursued as a job."
18. Willie Nelson and Kris Kristofferson
19. *The Restless Kind*
20. Marty Stuart

Shania Twain

Is there anyone out there these days who hasn't heard the sad stories of Shania Twain's childhood? It seems everyone you meet can relay the tales: She grew up poor in a large family, with a mom who was often so depressed she couldn't get out of bed. By age eight her parents were waking her up at one o'clock in the morning so she could sing in clubs after they'd stopped serving liquor. Her parents died in a car crash when Shania was just twenty-one, forcing Shania to abandon her singing career to care for her three younger siblings.

But while Shania will admit that her childhood was no bed of roses—"I pretty much missed my childhood. My career has always been very consuming," she says—this country diva prefers to savor the present rather than dwell on the past.

And who can blame her? These days, Shania is at the top of her game, having sold more than 17 million records worldwide. In fact, two of the three highest-selling albums ever issued by a female country artist are Shania's. Her videos have regular play on the pop and country music video channels, and her singles have consistently hit the top ten on the country and pop charts. On the personal front, Shania is happily married and living on a big spread in upstate New York. (She also has possibly the most famous belly button in country music, but that's another story.)

So just how much do you know about Shania? There's only one way to find out. You've got to take the quiz.

1. True or false: Shania grew up in Nashville.
2. Shania is an Ojibway Indian name meaning what?
3. What is Shania's real name?
4. Who is Shania's husband?
5. Which of the following is not one of Shania's hobbies: camping, skiing, surfing, or horseback riding?
6. True or false: Shania was once a foreman on a reforestation crew.
7. True or false: Shania is a heavy smoker.
8. What does Shania consider her worst trait?

9. How many siblings does Shania have?
10. True or false: Shania was discovered in Nashville.
11. Where has Shania said she would like to live by the year 2000, in order to increase her sense of privacy?
12. Name Shania's three horses.
13. Shania once sang background on which Sammy Kershaw tune?
14. Where did Shania and her husband first meet in person?
15. Why does Shania's husband call her Woody?
16. True or false: Shania's "Don't Be Stupid" video took six weeks to shoot.
17. Which Shania album won the 1996 Grammy for Best Country Album?
18. In 1998, Shania's "You're Still the One" won a VH1 Viewer's Award in which category?
19. What song did Shania sing in her first-grade play (which was her first live performance)?
20. Who produced *The Woman in Me* and *Come On Over?*
21. In 1998, Shania sold out Detroit's Pine Knob Theater in how many minutes?
        a. 67   b. 72   c. 29
22. What is the best-selling album by a female country artist?

23. How many CMA awards did Shania win in 1998?

24. Where did Shania film her "The Woman in Me" video?

25. With whom does Shania sing a duet on "From This Moment On"?

Answers to the Shania Twain Quiz

1. False—she grew up in Timmons, Ontario, Canada.
2. I'm on my way
3. Eileen Regina Twain
4. Record producer Robert "Mutt" Lange
5. Surfing
6. True
7. False—she is a nonsmoker.
8. Her impatience
9. Four—two sisters and two brothers. Shania is the second child.
10. False—her manager arranged for Nashville lawyer Richard Frank to hear Shania sing at a Canadian showcase.
11. Switzerland
12. Dancer, Star, and Tango
13. "Haunted Heart"
14. Fan Fair 1993
15. Because he thought her old hairdo made her look like Woody Woodpecker

16. False—it took only ten hours.
17. *The Woman in Me*
18. Sexiest Video
19. "Country Roads"
20. Mutt Lange
21. C—the tickets sold at a pace matched only by The Who, Metallica, Bob Seger, and Jimmy Buffett.
22. *The Woman in Me*
23. Six: Entertainer of the Year, Album of the Year, Female Artist of the Year, Single of the Year, Video of the Year, and Bestselling Album of the Year
24. Cairo, Egypt
25. Bryan White

Bryan White

When it comes to country music, *Billboard* magazine says "Bryan White is the real thing." And thousands of fans agree. Bryan's music is filled with the heart that country music has come to be known for. Still, some critics say that Bryan's sound leans a little toward pop music. And that's something Bryan's not apologizing for.

"People have to realize that younger artists didn't grow up in the traditional era," he explains. "We're open to so much more; we've been exposed to different kinds of music."

Bryan's unique sound is attracting new listeners to country music. By the end of 1998, he'd accumulated 5 number-one singles!

So, to what does Bryan attribute his great success? Some would argue his boyish good looks don't hurt, but Bryan says it's the music that brings in the fans.

"Making the song believable and deep is the most important thing," he insists. "I hope people understand that it's something I've put hard work into."

The hard work has certainly paid off. Bryan is now a certified country superstar, opening for big names like Pam Tillis and Vince Gill, and touring side-by-side with country dynamo LeAnn Rimes.

Now it's time to take a step in the *White* direction, and try your hand at these questions!

1. Where did Bryan debut his single "Love Is the Right Place"?
2. True or false: Bryan was once named one of *People* magazine's 50 most beautiful people.
3. Name the twins who opened for Bryan during some of the shows in his 1998 tour.
4. What do Bryan's songs "Someone Else's Love," "Rebecca Lynn," and "I'm Not Supposed to Love You Anymore" all have in common?
5. Which three fan magazines once named Bryan Country Teen Heartthrob of the Year?
6. Bryan hosted a benefit to provide schol-

arships for children orphaned or injured in what disaster?

7. Where did Bryan grow up?
8. True or false: Bryan's mom was a country singer.
9. True or false: Bryan plays drums.
10. What is Bryan's middle name?
11. What color are Bryan's eyes?
12. True or false: Bryan's self-titled debut CD never reached platinum status.
13. In 1995, Bryan won which ACM award?
14. What is Bryan's brother's name?
15. Finish the title of Bryan's second CD: *Between Now* _____.
16. What is Bryan's real hair color?
17. What was the first song Bryan ever learned?
18. What is Bryan's favorite song?
19. True or false: Bryan is a huge Greenbay Packers fan.
20. When choosing a song to perform, does Bryan consider the melody or lyrics first?
21. In what animated film can you hear Bryan's singing?
    a. *Mulan*   b. *Quest for Camelot*   c. *Antz*
22. True or false: Bryan considers himself a perfectionist.
23. Which of Bryan's singles was the first to crack the top forty?

24. True or false: Bryan wrote "Never Get Around to It," while in Oklahoma.
25. Which of the songs on *The Right Place* does Bryan believe to be similar to his huge number-one hit "Rebecca Lynn"?

Answers to the Bryan White Quiz

1. Onstage at the Grand Ole Opry
2. True
3. The Kinleys
4. They all went to number one.
5. *16, Tiger Beat,* and *Teen Beat*
6. The Oklahoma City bombing
7. Oklahoma City
8. False—she sang rock and rhythm and blues. His dad was the country singer.
9. True
10. Shelton
11. Green
12. False
13. Top New Male Vocalist
14. Daniel
15. *And Forever*
16. Brown
17. "Stand By Me"
18. "Behind Closed Doors" by Ray Charles
19. False—he's a Dallas Cowboys fan.
20. Melody

21. B
22. True
23. "Eugene You Genius"
24. False—he wrote it while on tour in Canada.
25. "Tree of Hearts"

Mark Wills

Mark Wills has been having growing pains recently. You can tell by listening to his latest songs. Mark's music is reflecting his newly found maturity. While his first, self-titled album was what he calls "a learning process for me to know what I want to do," Mark thinks his second album, *Wish You Were Here,* displays his more serious side.

If fans were happy with the old Mark, they seem to be ecstatic about the new version. *Wish You Were Here* gave Mark back-to-back number-one singles on the country charts.

With his youthful appeal and powerful video presence (and those brooding, dark eyes don't hurt, either!), Mark is bringing younger fans to the country world. So how does Mark feel about being a role model?

"That's scary," he admits. "I'm not finished growing up myself."

Still, as the music on *Wish You Were Here* proves, Mark's well on his way!

1. Mark is a native of what state?
2. Name Mark's first single, which spent 26 weeks on the charts.
3. Finish Mark's famous quote about his music: "Music is my way of _____."
4. Mark records for what label?
5. Who is Mally Ann?
6. Which instruments does Mark play?
7. What is Mark's middle name?
8. What is the name of Mark's band?
9. What was the first single from Mark's *Wish You Were Here* album?
10. Complete this lyric from "Jacob's Ladder":
    Head over heels for a brown-eyed girl,
    And gettin' caught _____.
11. Name Mark's sister and foster brother.
12. Complete this lyric from "Don't Laugh at Me":
    I'm a little boy with glasses
    The one they call geek.
    A little girl who never smiles
    'Cause _____.
13. Finish the title of this song from *Wish You Were Here:* "Anywhere but _____."

14. Name the famous director who worked with Mark on the video for "I Do (Cherish You)."
15. True or false: Mark is shy and shuns attention.

Answers to the Mark Wills Quiz

1. Georgia
2. "Jacob's Ladder"
3. Communicating
4. Mercury
5. Mark's daughter
6. Drums and guitar
7. Mark—his full name is Daryl Mark Williams.
8. Nokintobob (No kin to Bob)
9. "I Do (Cherish You)"
10. Didn't seem to matter
11. Amy and Teo
12. I've got braces on my teeth
13. Memphis
14. Peter Zavadil
15. False—in fact, Mark says, "I love the attention. Anybody that's in this business may tell you they don't, but they do."

Lee Ann Womack

Lee Ann Womack has a slight problem. It seems people sometimes get her confused with that other LeAnn—LeAnn Rimes. At one point her record label even considered asking Lee Ann to change her name to avoid the confusion. But Decca Records really had nothing to worry about. The minute you hear Lee Ann Womack's music, you realize that the two are very different artists.

While LeAnn Rimes has a sound that's forced its way to the top of both the pop and country charts, Lee Ann Womack is pure country. Traditional country. The kind of music that makes you feel like you're going home.

There aren't many women singing traditional country anymore, and that's distressing to Lee Ann. "It's kind of sad to me that there are not more people doing traditional country music," she admits. "That is where we came from. But at least I get to do country music and the irony of it is at the same time be different."

The fans love Lee Ann's traditional sound, and so do her fellow country singers. Alan Jackson liked her debut album so much that he bought twenty-five copies and put them in every car, boat, bus, and truck he owns.

How much do you know about this Lee Ann? There's no time like the present to find out!

1. True or false: Lee Ann was on the tennis team at her high school.
2. Lee Ann won her first American Music Award in what category?
3. What country superstar has been quoted as saying that Lee Ann came closer to her style of singing than any other new female artist?
4. What did Lee Ann major in at South Plains Junior College?
5. Who is Lee Ann's favorite cartoon character?
6. What does Lee Ann say was her favorite Christmas gift ever?
7. Lee Ann once interned in the A&R department at what record company?
8. Lee Ann got her start in the business as a staff writer for what music publisher?

9. What is Lee Ann's favorite food?
10. What does Lee Ann consider her favorite career moment?
11. What is Lee Ann's nickname?
12. Name Lee Ann's debut single.
13. What is Lee Ann's favorite TV show?
14. What did Lee Ann's father do for a living?
15. True or false: Lee Ann's daughter Aubrie goes to boarding school in London while her mother is touring.

Answers to the Lee Ann Womack Quiz

1. True, but she quit to become a cheerleader.
2. Most Promising Country Artist
3. Loretta Lynn
4. Bluegrass and country music
5. Foghorn Leghorn
6. Her first stereo
7. MCA
8. Tree Publishing
9. Her mother's biscuits (Her least favorite food is her own biscuits.)
10. The day she signed with Decca Records
11. Lu

12. "Never Again, Again"
13. The *Andy Griffith Show*
14. He was a part-time disc jockey
15. False—Aubrie is home-schooled by her mom, and travels on the bus when Lee Ann goes on tour.

Trisha Yearwood

You don't get more country than Trisha Yearwood. She's a simple, down-home, southern girl who describes herself as being "as country as biscuit."

Still, Trisha's sound has managed to find a home with pop audiences. But unlike some of her contemporaries who have also had pop hits, Trisha hasn't lost any of her country fans in the process. Maybe that's because Trisha hasn't consciously gone out and tried to make it in the pop world. It's just something that happened.

"I think my fans are with me because my music has simply evolved. But it isn't changing drastically," she recently told *TV Guide*. "My music still feels country to me."

And that's how her music feels to her millions of fans, too!

1. With which famous opera performer did Trisha perform "O Come, All Ye Faithful"?

2. Trisha was once a receptionist at a record label owned by what TV star?

3. Trisha's husband, Robert Reynolds, plays bass for what group?

4. What song did Trisha perform at the 1998 Academy Awards?

5. What does Trisha say is the most difficult part of her career?

6. Trisha grew up on a farm in which southern state?

7. What was Trisha's major at Belmont University?

8. Trisha's first single shot all the way to number eleven. Name it.

9. How many hit singles did the CD *Trisha Yearwood* spawn?

10. Name Trisha's Christmas album.

11. True or false: Trisha's greatest hits package, *Song Book,* debuted at number one on the *Billboard* charts.

12. In what southern state does Trisha now live?

13. Who is Roseanne?

14. Who was Trisha's first musical idol?

15. On her first major tour, Trisha opened for what major country superstar?

16. *Thinkin' About You* was released on what holiday in 1995?

17. Trisha gave a percentage of the sales from *Thinkin' About You* to what charity?

18. Who runs Trisha's fan club?

19. With whom did Trisha duet on "In Another's Eyes"?

20. With whom did Trisha sing a duet on "Walkaway Joe"?

21. In 1994 Trisha won a Grammy for her duet with Aaron Neville. Name the song.

22. Who wrote "To Make You Feel My Love," Trisha's contribution to the *Hope Floats* sound track?

23. Trisha sang, "How Do I Live" for which movie's sound track?

24. What was the first debut album by a female country artist ever to surpass sales of a million copies?

25. "Bring Me All Your Lovin'" is Trisha's tribute to what band?

Answers to the Trisha Yearwood Quiz

1. Luciano Pavarotti
2. Mary Tyler Moore's MTM Records
3. The Mavericks
4. "How Do I Live"
5. Performing

6. Georgia
7. Business administration (music business)
8. "She's in Love with the Boy"
9. Four
10. *The Sweetest Gift*
11. True
12. Tennessee
13. Trisha's dog, whom she named for her favorite TV character
14. Elvis Presley
15. Garth Brooks
16. Valentine's Day
17. The American Heart Association
18. Her parents
19. Garth Brooks
20. Don Henley
21. "I Fall to Pieces"
22. Bob Dylan
23. *Con Air*
24. *Trisha Yearwood*
25. The Rolling Stones

Dwight Yoakam

Have you ever done The Dwight? You just put your legs together, bend your knees, twist down, and twist up again.

The Dwight is a really simple dance move, which is kind of ironic, because Dwight Yoakam (whom the dance is named for) is an extremely complicated performer. He's a perfectionist who finds true happiness in every little detail of his work. That kind of complexity shows itself not only in Dwight's songs; it's also evident in the way he pours himself into the characters he has portrayed in films such as *Sling Blade, The Newton Boys,* and *When Trumpets Fade.*

Although Dwight has been recording for more than twelve years now, these days he has been spending quite a bit of time in front of movie cameras, and many of his fans have been concerned that he was going "Hollywood." But they can relax. Dwight is determined to stick to his country music roots—even though he's moved his home to Los Angeles. Dwight still considers himself the same down-home boy whose early music was considered by some to be too pure country for the Grand Ole Opry.

And don't worry that acting will someday overshadow Dwight's music. That will never happen. Dwight needs music as badly as he needs to act. The two fulfill completely separate needs for this multi-talented artist.

"Music is very personal," he explains. "It's an exploration of my very soul. Superficially, acting allows me to escape myself, although ultimately I strike some pretty personal chords."

How much do you know about the personal (and professional) world of Dwight Yoakam? You don't have to take the *Long Road Home* to find out. The questions are right here.

1. Dwight once performed at Hollywood's House of Blues with legendary pop star Tom Jones. What song did the two do as a duet?

2. Dwight's HBO movie *When Trumpets Fade* took place during which war?

3. What kind of food bears Dwight's name?

4. In which film did Dwight play evil

Doyle Hargraves?

   a. *When Trumpets Fade*   b. *Sling Blade*   c. *The Newton Boys*

5. In which state was Dwight born?

6. True or false: Dwight is an only child.

7. What was Dwight's major during his short stay at Ohio State University?

8. True or false: There's a highway named for Dwight.

9. Why did Dwight neglect to bring a guitar to the three-month location shoot of *The Newton Boys?*

10. Which of his albums did Dwight describe as "Late 20th century fastback muscle car country music"?

11. What famous actor interviewed Dwight during his Disney Channel special, *Dwight Live?*

12. What music legends appear with Dwight on the "Streets of Bakersfield" video?

13. Which of these is not one of Dwight's idols: Elvis Presley, Roy Rogers, Johnny Cash, or Roy Orbison?

14. Who originally recorded "Baby Don't Go"?

15. True or false: Dwight wrote "Try Not to Look So Pretty" for his ex—Sharon Stone.

16. Proceeds from the sale of which Dwight Yoakam album went to the homeless?

17. With whom did Dwight do a duet on Hammer and Lace Records' *Hollywood Goes Wild?*

18. How old was Dwight when he wrote his first song?

19. What color is Dwight's Stetson?

20. How tall is Dwight?

21. Name the clothing company Dwight owns.

22. How old was Dwight when he began playing guitar?

23. What was the name of Dwight's first independent EP?

24. Complete this line from "A Thousand Miles from Nowhere":

    I got heartaches in my pocket
    I got echoes in my head
    And all that I keep hearing
    Are the _____.

25. For what song did Dwight win the 1993 Grammy?

Answers to the Dwight Yoakam Quiz

1. "The Last Time"
2. World War II
3. Dwight Yoakam's Bakersfield Biscuits
4. B
5. Kentucky

6. False—he's the eldest of three. His siblings are named Ronald and Kimberly.
7. Philosophy and history
8. True—it's a stretch of highway along U.S. 23 (the Country Music Highway), which runs through Floyd County, KY.
9. He wanted to spend the time preparing for his role.
10. *A Long Way Home*
11. Dennis Hopper
12. Buck Owens and Flaco Jimenez
13. Roy Rogers
14. Sonny and Cher
15. False
16. *Dwight Yoakam: Will Sing for Food*
17. Billy Bob Thornton
18. Nine—the song was called "How Far Is Heaven?"
19. White
20. Six feet
21. DY Ranchwear
22. Six
23. *A Town South of Bakersfield*
24. Cruel, cruel, things you said
25. "Ain't That Lonely Yet"

The *Pop Quiz* Country Music Hall of Fame Quiz

Patsy Cline. Conway Twitty. Merle Haggard. Tammy Wynette. Charlie Pride. Loretta Lynn. Johnny Cash.

These artists may not have albums in the top ten these days, but you can still hear them everywhere you turn. Listen closely to the songs of today's hottest country superstars and you'll hear their influences loud and clear.

How much do you know about the superstars who truly put the Grand in the Grand Ole Opry? Take this quiz and find out.

Patsy Cline

1. Which of Patsy's recordings became the number-one jukebox hit of all time?
2. What was Patsy's real name?

3. On what show did Patsy make her TV debut?
4. True or false: Patsy's recording of "Pieces" reached number one on the country and pop charts.
5. How old was Patsy when she died in a plane crash in 1963?

Conway Twitty

6. How many of Conway's number-one hits did he write himself?
7. What was Conway's real name?
8. How did Conway come up with his professional name?
9. Name Conway's first number-one hit.
10. What nickname did Jerry Clower bestow on Conway?

Merle Haggard

11. True or false: Merle once spent time in jail.
12. Name Merle's first album.
13. How many number-one songs has Merle had?
14. When did Merle become a member of the Country Music Hall of Fame?
15. Merle once walked off only minutes be-

fore he was scheduled to perform on
what famed variety show?

Tammy Wynette

16. Tammy was raised by her grandparents
    on what kind of farm?
17. In a 1968 single, Tammy spelled out
    what type of relationship demise?
18. Tammy and which of her husbands were
    dubbed "The President and First Lady
    of Country Music"?
19. Who co-wrote "Stand By Your Man"
    with Tammy?
20. "Stand By Your Man" was featured in
    what Jack Nicholson film?

Charlie Pride

21. True or false: Charlie was once a profes-
    sional baseball player.
22. What was Charlie's first song to hit the
    top ten?
23. How many number-one country hits has
    Charlie had?
24. In what year was Charlie named the
    CMA Entertainer of the Year?
25. In what year was Charlie first asked to
    join the Grand Ole Opry?

Loretta Lynn

26. How old was Loretta when she married?
27. Name Loretta's first single.
28. In what three years was Loretta named the CMA's Entertainer of the Year?
29. What is considered Loretta's signature song?
30. What was Loretta's first number-one single with Conway Twitty?

Johnny Cash

31. In what year was Johnny elected into the CMA Hall of Fame?
32. Johnny's hit recording of "A Boy Named Sue" was recorded at what prison?
33. Which of the famed Carter Sisters did Johnny marry in 1968?
34. What did Johnny host from 1969–1971?
35. True or false: Johnny is a member of both the Country Music Hall of Fame and the Rock and Roll Hall of Fame.

Dolly Parton

36. How many siblings does Dolly have?
37. Who bought Dolly her first guitar?
38. How old was Dolly when she made her

first guest appearance on the stage of the Grand Ole Opry?

39. Name the theme park founded by Dolly.
40. Which of Dolly's compositions did Whitney Houston take to number one in 1992?

Kitty Wells

41. Kitty was the first female country singer to earn what award?
42. Finish the title of Kitty's famous song: "It Wasn't God Who _____."
43. Where was Kitty born?
44. Who did Kitty marry in 1937?
45. How many top-ten singles did Kitty record?

Charlie Rich

46. Charlie was in which branch of the armed forces when he played with the Velvetones?
47. What did Charlie do to the Entertainer of the Year award envelope at the 1973 CMA awards ceremony?
48. In 1973, Charlie had a country, pop, and international hit with what song?
49. Name the first label Charlie ever signed with.

50. What spot did "A Very Special Love Song" reach on the *Billboard* country charts?

Willie Nelson

51. True or false: Willie was once a radio DJ.
52. Name Willie's first single, released in 1962.
53. Where did Willie hold his famed "Willie Nelson Picnics"?
54. In what Robert Redford film did Willie appear?
55. *To Lefty from Willie* is Willie Nelson's tribute to whom?

Tanya Tucker

56. How old was Tanya when she released "Delta Dawn" in 1972?
57. What is the name of Tanya's autobiography?
58. What was the only Tanya Tucker song to crack the pop music top forty?
59. How many top-ten hits did "Girl Like Me" yield for Tanya?
60. With whom did Tanya sing the duet "Dream Lover"?

Waylon Jennings

61. Waylon Jennings was just a teenager when he played bass for what rock and roll legend?
62. Name Waylon's first record.
63. True or false: When Waylon first moved to Nashville, his roommate was Willie Nelson.
64. In what movie did Waylon star in 1966?
65. True or false: Waylon once pulled out a pistol in a recording studio.

Reba McEntire

66. Name Reba's first top-twenty single.
67. What number did "How Blue" reach on the country charts?
68. What was the first movie Reba appeared in?
69. In 1991, seven members of Reba's band died. How did that happen?
70. What was the singing group Reba and her siblings formed?

The Carter Sisters

71. Name the three Carter sisters.
72. True or false: The Carter Sisters once opened for Elvis Presley.

73. True or false: Anita sometimes stood on one leg to play the bass.
74. Which of the Carter sisters studied at The Actors Studio?
75. Whose memoir is *From the Heart?*

Hank Williams

76. What spinal problem was Hank born with?
77. Hank's first hit was called "Lovesick _____."
78. Who was Luke the Drifter?
79. Who made a hit record of Hank's "Cold, Cold Heart"?
80. Who made a hit of Hank's "Hey Good Lookin' "?

Eddy Arnold

81. What is Eddy Arnold's full name?
82. What was Eddy's professional nickname?
83. Eddy was a featured singer with what group?
84. Eddy shared his manager with what rock and roll legend?
85. Eddy was the first country star to play Las Vegas. What hotel did he appear at?

Jimmie Rogers

86. Jimmie holds what honor with the Country Music Hall of Fame?
87. What were Jimmie's two professional nicknames?
88. How old was Jimmie when he won a talent contest and ran away with a traveling medicine show?
89. When Jimmie sang with the Tennessee Ramblers, what were they known as?
90. What was *The Singing Brakeman?*

Chet Atkins

91. What did Chet's father do for a living?
92. What was Chet's first solo recording?
93. What was Chet's first song to make the charts?
94. In what year was Chet elected to the Country Music Hall of Fame?
95. In 1993 Chet won a Lifetime Achievement Award from what organization?

Answers to the *Pop Quiz*
Country Music Hall of Fame Quiz

1. "Crazy"
2. Virginia Patterson Hensley
3. *Arthur Godfrey's Talent Scouts*

4. False—it was number one on the country charts and number twelve on the pop charts.
5. Thirty
6. Eleven
7. Harold Lloyd Jenkins
8. He combined the towns of Conway, AR, and Twitty, TX.
9. "Next in Line"
10. The High Priest of Country Music
11. True—for theft and writing bad checks
12. *Strangers*
13. Thirty-eight
14. 1994
15. *The Ed Sullivan Show*
16. A cotton farm
17. "D-I-V-O-R-C-E"
18. George Jones
19. Billy Sherrill
20. *Five Easy Pieces*
21. True—he played in the Negro American League and the Pioneer League.
22. "Just Between You and Me"
23. Twenty-nine
24. 1971
25. 1968—but he declined. He became a cast member in 1993.
26. Thirteen
27. "I'm a Honky Tonk Girl"

28. 1967, 1972, and 1973
29. "Coal Miner's Daughter"
30. "After the Fire Is Gone"
31. 1980
32. San Quentin
33. June Carter
34. His own prime-time network TV variety show
35. True
36. Eleven
37. Her uncle, Bill Owens
38. Thirteen
39. Dollywood
40. "I Will Always Love You"
41. The Grammy Lifetime Achievement Award
42. Made Honky-Tonk Angels
43. Nashville, TN
44. Country singer Johnny Wright
45. Thirty-eight
46. The air force
47. He set it on fire. (The name in the envelope was John Denver.)
48. "Behind Closed Doors"
49. Sun Records
50. Number one
51. True
52. "Touch Me"
53. Dripping Springs, TX
54. *The Electric Horseman*

55. Lefty Frizzell
56. Thirteen
57. *Nickel Dreams, My Life*
58. "Lizzie and the Rainman"
59. Four
60. Glen Campbell
61. Buddy Holly
62. *Jole Blon*
63. False—his roommate was Johnny Cash.
64. *Nashville Rebel*
65. True—he did it to protest studio bullying by RCA.
66. "Sweet Dreams"
67. Number one
68. *Tremors*
69. They were in a plane crash.
70. The Singing McEntires
71. Helen Myrl, Valerie June, Ina Anita
72. True
73. False—but she did sometimes stand on her head.
74. June
75. June Carter Cash's
76. Spina bifida oculta
77. Blues
78. Hank Williams (It was a pseudonym he used when recording talking blues songs.)
79. Tony Bennett
80. Frankie Laine and Jo Stafford

81. Richard Edward Arnold
82. The Tennessee Plowboy
83. PeeWee King's Golden West Cowboys
84. Elvis Presley—the manager was Tom Parker.
85. The Sahara Hotel
86. He was the first performer inducted into the Hall of Fame.
87. The Singing Brakeman and America's Blue Yodeler
88. Thirteen
89. The Jimmie Rodgers Entertainers
90. A fifteen-minute short film that Jimmie starred in
91. He was a music teacher.
92. "Guitar Blues"
93. "Mr. Sandman"
94. 1973
95. The National Academy of Recording Arts and Sciences

How Country Are You?!

Okay, everybody! This is the moment you've been waiting for. We're about to find out if you are truly the ultimate country fan!

There are **800** questions in this book. To get your score, go through each quiz, and count how many questions you answered correctly. Then total up your number of correct answers. Finally, check the chart below to see how you measure up.

680–800 correct: Whew! We're gonna induct you into the Grand Ole Opry—as the most amazing fan!

500–679 correct: Congratulations. With a score this great, we're handing you the key to Music City.

350–499 correct: Nice score. You can wear your cowboy boots with pride!

150–349 correct: Whoops, you're slipping. It's time to drive over to your local country music dance club and listen to some tunes. (Enjoy a few line dances while you're there, too!)

0–149 correct: Yikes! You are in need of a country music refresher course. Start with your CDs, move over to TNN, and then try your luck again.

About the Author

Nancy E. Krulik is a freelance writer who is the author of several trivia books including *Pop Quiz* and *Pop Quiz: Leonardo DiCaprio*. She has also written celebrity biographies including the *New York Times* best-sellers *Leonardo DiCaprio: A Biography* and *Taylor Hanson: Totally Taylor!*

DON'T MISS ANY OF OUR
BEST-SELLING POP MUSIC BIOS!

Backstreet Boys ☆ Aaron Carter
by Matt Netter

Five
by Matt Netter

Dancin' With Hanson
by Ravi

Hanson: Mmmbop to the Top
by Jill Matthews

Isaac Hanson: Totally Ike!
by Nancy Krulik

Taylor Hanson: Totally Taylor!
by Nancy Krulik

Zac Hanson: Totally Zac!
by Matt Netter

Hanson: The Ultimate Trivia Book
by Matt Netter

Jewel: Pieces of a Dream
by Kristen Kemp

Pop Quiz
by Nancy Krulik

'N Sync: Tearin' Up the Charts
by Matt Netter

Will Smith: Will Power!
by Jan Berenson